W0246984

The Power of You

THE

POWER

OF

YOU

Manifest Your Wildest Dreams in Seven Steps

MICHELE KNIGHT-WAITE

JOHN MURRAY

First published in Great Britain by John Murray One in 2025
An imprint of John Murray Press

SRD

Copyright © Michele Knight-Waite 2025

The right of Michele Knight-Waite to be identified as the Author of the Work
has been asserted by her in accordance with the Copyright,
Designs and Patents Act 1988.

All rights reserved. No part of this publication may be reproduced, stored in a
retrieval system, or transmitted, in any form or by any means without the prior
written permission of the publisher, nor be otherwise circulated in any form of
binding or cover other than that in which it is published and without a similar
condition being imposed on the subsequent purchaser.

A CIP catalogue record for this title is available from the British Library

Hardback ISBN 978 1 399 81037 1
ebook ISBN 978 1 399 81039 5

Typeset by KnowledgeWorks Global Ltd.

Printed and bound in India by Manipal Technologies Limited, Manipal

John Murray Press policy is to use papers that are natural, renewable and recyclable
products and made from wood grown in sustainable forests. The logging and
manufacturing processes are expected to conform to the environmental
regulations of the country of origin.

John Murray Press
Carmelite House
50 Victoria Embankment
London EC4Y 0DZ

John Murray Press
123 S. Broad St., Ste 2750
Philadelphia, PA 19109

www.johnmurraypress.co.uk

John Murray Press, part of Hodder & Stoughton Limited
An Hachette UK company

MIX
Paper | Supporting
responsible forestry
FSC
www.fsc.org   FSC™ C104740

Dedicated to my wife, co-creator, and inspiration
Cathy Knight-Waite

CONTENTS

INTRODUCTION

Been There, Done That – Got Nothing?

Before we begin: have you tried manifesting – and zilch?

Have you been dreaming, longing, and wishing for a better future? Have you thrown yourself into manifesting, vision boarded like a wild thing, religiously carried crystals in your underwear while lighting your New Moon candles and chanting positive affirmations, and yet nada, nix, nothing?

Or perhaps there's been the occasional near-miss? The charming lover who ticks every box until you discover they are a compulsive liar? That dream job which turns into a nightmare thanks to that micromanaging and snarky boss? Don't worry, you're not alone. And we're going to look at the reasons why.

So, Just Why Hasn't It Happened?

Seeking further guidance, you pored over the multitude of manifesting posts on Instagram. Devoured one of the thousands of manifesting podcasts and binged those YouTube channels. You ordered a plethora of self-help and visualization books. And the only thing you've taken away from all of this is the message that it is all your fault. Yes, you created your present circumstances. Your vibes were off. And your flawed thinking is solely responsible for your challenging situation. Or your lack of results.

First, those kinds of negative messages are not only incorrect, they will hinder your efforts to create the life you deserve. Second, and let me be really clear about this: you are not a failure. You are not to blame if bad things happen. We don't just individually order; we are impacted by the collective and those around us. No, it is not your fault if your manifesting desires haven't yet arrived. Your 'negative' thoughts are not responsible. Nobody can think positively all the time. That's impossible – and unrealistic. Ask any psychologist. And no, your focus, dedication, or willpower aren't at fault either. In fact, none of this is.

Here's a radical idea I want to introduce: you were doing nothing wrong. As we begin our journey together, I want you to understand that you are lovable, worthy, and equal to anyone on this earth. One of the reasons I took my time in writing this book is because a lot of people who talk about manifesting don't take into account social injustice, situations in the world where people are struggling to survive, let alone in a position to be able to manifest; and they don't take in account different kinds of oppression, which can make it harder. There are some terrible things going on in the world; there are people who are dealing with constant negative group projections: racism, homophobia, etc. We have to collectively help each other and stay aware. Indeed, it is our collective duty to do so.

Know this: wherever you come from and whatever you have experienced, you are a perfect soul. There is nothing flawed about you. Look around you and find others who have the kind of life you yearn for and imagine yourself leading. They are not 'better' than you or more deserving than you. And if they can live the life of their dreams, then take it from me, so can you. The fact you have this book in your hands tells you that it is now your time to break through and tap into your huge reservoirs of magic and self-certainty. And receive what you truly desire. And by the end of this book, it can be your very own story of success.

Yes, there's work to be done, but believe me, it's not hard. And you already have what it takes to do it. That's the miracle you're about to embrace. That nothing is going to be asked of you that you don't already have or are naturally adept at doing. No matter what you may have been made to believe. Because manifesting isn't something that is available to a few, select 'gifted' people but a conduit to the Universe that anyone can access. And I am about to show you exactly how.

Ready to begin your journey? It's going to be a wild ride that takes you to places you never imagined. So, hold that dream and climb aboard!

PART 1
THE JOURNEY

CHAPTER 1

MY STORY

As I write this, I am sitting at my writing desk in a small, white log cabin next to my vegetable garden. Looking out through its stained-glass window, I see a Gothic castle. Its turret rising above the trees, the sun glinting off the huge windows at the front, leading out into the gardens. The castle overlooks a field where rescue donkeys graze and then out onto the wild blue Devon sea.

It is my castle.

So how did I get from being homeless when I was six months pregnant to living this reality? Ever since childhood, I carried a weird certainty and inner knowing that my destiny was a castle. Running around with a toy sword, I vowed to have my own turret one day. The difference between my childhood fantasy and others is that I never let it go. Even at 20, a single mother in a council flat, I created my castle-like refuge. I painted the walls gloss red, decorated them with gilded frames found in charity shops, and dreamed of the day my vision would become reality. Despite a limited budget, I traveled across the UK whenever I could, visiting castles and unknowingly turning my humble flat into a living vision board for my desires. I even went one step further, changing my surname to Knight!

Since achieving my dream (and even before), I've been committed to sharing my journey and my knowledge of manifesting. I've held workshops since I was 21 and written endless articles and made videos about it. Thirty-seven years later the time has come to write an easy-to-understand Manifesting Manual to

3

give you all the knowledge I have to achieve happiness and fulfillment, and perhaps your own childhood dreams.

I couldn't be more excited to share how to transform your life and to manifest your wildest and most intense desires. To take you through the steps that took me from being homeless and broken, to living the abundant and love-filled life I have now.

Yes, I encountered many painful experiences along the way, which made me wiser and more determined to pursue my destiny. Reading this, you might think of me as lucky. But I can assure you, the 'luck' came from the steps I'm going to share. Most importantly, these are the pivotal moments that led to the breakthroughs that honed the steps in this book. So, I know firsthand that these work.

So, let's start at the beginning. I was born into a tempestuous yet magical household, having inherited my psychic abilities from my Italian mother, whose healing circles I joined at the age of three. Tarot cards were my playthings and a belief in magic was normal. There were regular seances. Strange and interesting characters would line up on the doorstep for a reading with my fiery, chain-smoking mother. Indeed, my mum said she manifested me after 20 years of trying – and that I was conceived via a wish she made on an Egyptian scarab beetle my father had brought back from one of his work trips. So you see, my childhood was anything but 'normal'.

My father was dying when I was born and passed away when I was five, leaving my mother in dire financial straits. I rarely saw her after that as she worked as a carer at night and a psychic during the day. Although we lived in a nice house that my dad had bought, unaware that he was dying, we were so poor we lacked all the things other families had.

It's fair to say I was not the most popular of kids growing up. Reading palms in the school toilets and talking about reincarnation at ten earned me no friends and led to me being labeled a 'weirdo'. On top of that, I was chunky, scruffy, and unapologetically fierce. I got called Tank or Tubby Dread. I was very lonely. Plus, there was another issue adding to my feeling of being apart or an outsider: I didn't have a bike. Every other kid had one. It was a symbol of belonging and being able to socialize. Not having one made me feel even more excluded.

Unsurprisingly, my first conscious attempt at manifesting involved a red Chopper bike. I did not care that due to our dire financial situation, it was impossible. I heard on the childhood wonder grapevine that if you wished on a dandelion seed, it would float up and be delivered to the powers that be. I totally believed this was possible. So, off I went, scooping up the dandelions and blowing with all my might, watching the seeds fly away on the wind as I saw myself cycling in the local park on my Chopper of Dreams, dressed in my flared jeans and cross medallion.

I then moved on with the absolute conviction that my Chopper was on the way. Little did I know that I naturally put into place the important steps to manifesting. Within a few weeks, I woke up to a red Chopper at the end of my bed. My mother had got it on tick from a catalog. That Chopper was my happiest memory from my childhood. And from that point on, I would occasionally manifest something else. And one way or another, it would appear. The key was, I HAD TO BELIEVE IT. If I had any doubt, it failed to materialize. The other problem was that in my wild youth, I didn't know what to ask for, and I didn't necessarily choose wisely.

My childhood was largely unsupervised. My early years were punctuated with violence, mayhem, and trauma. My fiery Aries nature made me crave independence – because surely I could take care of myself better than this? I needed to live my truth. I came out as a lesbian and left home at 13. Was briefly in a children's home, until I moved into a women's squat in Brixton, South London, as a young, political, punk rebel at the ripe old age of 15. Looking back, I wonder how I came through this period in one piece. That's a miracle in itself.

It was the 80s. We had great music, Doc Marten boots, and we survived on the food we found on the street at Brixton Market. But the squat was so damp that I occasionally woke up with slugs crawling across my purple Mohican. Grim! Living with a bunch of wild, creative women in a community gave me a happiness and sense of friendship and family I had never known (as well as drama and some tough lessons). And dream of dreams, I would give Tarot readings, and we would have Moon meditations during which I shared the magical techniques I grew up with. All things witchy were in. Suddenly, all the quirks that had made me different were considered valuable and attractive. I threw myself into the study and practice of manifesting, crystals, Tarot, and astrology with full force and accepted my pathway in life.

At 19, I got pregnant, and at six months I was homeless and breaking into squats in Holborn, central London. Intent on securing a flat for my baby, I sent out my manifesting desire (minus dandelion seeds!) and sure enough, within a couple of months, I was living in a council flat in Euston, central London. Despite the fact that the average wait for a council flat in those days could be as long as five years. Okay, we didn't have any furniture and the cot was on the floor, but we had made it. Manifesting had worked for me once more.

At the age of 21 I started running workshops on areas such as psychic development and creating your destiny. My next big manifestation was a life-changing one. I was inspired by a client of my mother who decided to have a Tarot reading with me. *Christine was a fearless American in her 40s. She had also led a tempestuous life. And she talked to me about quantum physics and her belief in manifesting.

Christine traveled the world and lived in a multi-million-pound house. She had several readings with me and I told her that one of my big dreams was to go to America. As a single parent on benefits, this should have been impossible. But a week later, I was on a plane to LA, staying at the Sunset Marquis and sitting next to Bruce Springsteen, while watching Dave Stewart from the Eurythmics walk past me. (And slightly perturbed as I was pretty sure I had wanted to manifest meeting Annie Lennox!) Which just goes to show that one can manifest, but your order might be slightly different from what you expected.

Having had deep conversations on the plane with Christine about her beliefs, I was even more committed to creating solid foundations for my future. At the time, Christine appeared to be several steps ahead of me. And one day, she asked me: *Where do you want an office in London?* I immediately replied: Covent Garden. We jumped into a taxi and I kid you not, within two hours I had a practically rent-free office in Endell Street, Covent Garden. Christine and I walked into an unleased space with

---

* All identifying names have been changed.

several shop units and Christine informed the owner: 'This is one of the best psychics in London. Give her the shop for free and she will give you a cut of all her readings.' Boom! I ended up having reasonably rented offices in Covent Garden for over a decade, which brought to me all manner of fascinating characters and opportunities.

I wanted to share this with you so you will know, if I can do it – you can do it! You can find peace, happiness, and fulfillment. In this book, I will share all the techniques, knowledge, and magic I learned along the way. Taking you through it step by step, so that you too can experience the marvel of manifestation. And live the life of your dreams.

It was my unconventional background that gave me the unique and unexpected gift that is essential to manifesting. TO BELIEVE IT IS POSSIBLE. Regardless of how tough things were, or what hideous things happened to me, nothing could shake my belief in magic and the power to manifest. And you can too.

We are meant to use our immense potential and energy to create a life of joy, abundance, and passion. This book is my gift to you. Manifest with love.

CHAPTER 2

THIS IS FOR YOU

From the early 90s, I became obsessed with discovering the deeper meaning of life. And how quantum physics and spirituality appeared to merge in so many ways. I've spent over 30 years studying, writing, and running workshops about manifesting and what I used to call 'Quantum Creating'. It formed the foundation for the basis of this book. If I'm honest, I was trying to find a way to 'prove' why it works. Yet the key to manifesting is letting go, trusting and experiencing the evidence with your own eyes. You don't need to understand how it works, but I found studying the metaphors and science made it easier to believe and to let go – and let flow.

My goal with this book is to distill all the processes and knowledge that have worked for me into one clear, accessible format. And to hand you every tool, secret, and process that I've learned on my journey. Broken down into simple steps so that you can get the results you deserve. Because my goal is for you to be able to create your own unique, distinctive, and fulfilled reality, which comes prepackaged with love and inspiring experiences tailored specifically to your dreams.

I believe we are all a distinctive and unrepeatable spark of the Universe. And that each one of us has special skills and magic encoded within us – like DNA of our souls. Finding the way to access this releases our ability to make our dreams come true. The trick to manifesting is finding the technique that works for you.

This book is designed to give you those techniques. So that you can easily and simply draw toward you the life that you deserve.

9

And most importantly, create a better relationship with yourself, with others, and with the outside world along the way.

The Utimate Manifesting Steps

You'll uncover seven simple yet magical manifestation principles to help you create the life of your dreams. Plus, I've included a special soul kit of additional tools that will supercharge your manifestation abilities in the later chapters.

The Steps

Step One Unleash Your Unique Soul
Step Two Believe It Is Possible and Know You Deserve It
Step Three Write Your Manifesting Manifesto
Step Four Order With the Joy and Expectation of a Child
Step Five Connect With Your Future Self
Step Six Embrace Co-Creation Power
Step Seven Light Your Soul Lamp

These open up a portal of possibility. One that resides within you. But which you may not have been able to fully access before. Each one builds on the previous one. And each one is designed to fire up your authentic soul and reconnect you to your power. The power of you!

Having said that, it's important to check under our hoods. What are we already calling in? Maybe without even knowing it? So, as part of each step, we'll check there is nothing getting between you and what you desire to bring into being. Anything from the detoxing ideas and beliefs that could potentially be holding you back to an all-out deep cleanse of your psyche. We're going to remove any blocks between you and your desires, leaving you clear and ready to receive exactly what you ordered. These secret recipes to success will be woven into each of the seven steps.

TIP

No matter what you order, make space and KNOW the Universe can bring in something even better.

Turn On, Tune In, Set Your Wavelength

As we begin, we need to check our frequency and our core beliefs. Why? Because we might be sending out mixed signals and not even know it. These are colored by our previous experiences, the people around us – partners past and present, teachers, friends and family, our society, the media – and even what has been passed down from our ancestors. All feed into our beliefs about the world we live in, what is possible, who we are, and our worth.

For example, you might want to attract love but deep down feel that you are unlovable or unworthy of the kind of love you yearn for. You unconsciously send out a mixed message along the lines of 'I want a loving, committed relationship, but the thought terrifies me because I've been hurt before, so please make sure I don't get it'. Often this can result in us attracting a partner who is emotionally unavailable to us in some way. (I did this many times in the past.)

In fact, we can end up with a string of these kinds of relationships. Where the person we attract is unavailable to us – the lover who blows hot and cold, who breadcrumbs us, the married lover, the long-distance lover, the workaholic. If you recognize this pattern in your life, be kind to yourself. You have developed it out of self-protection. But you no longer need to do that. Imagine instead what it would feel like to trust the Universe and trust yourself to bring you what you need. Feel your heart whole, open, and free. Now you're ready.

Perhaps what you want to attract is abundance instead. But that internal tape that's been running since your childhood is a loop which tells you that life's a struggle, money is hard to come by/the root of all evil, and good things can't really happen for you. Or if they did, something bad would ensure that you lost it again anyway.

It's contradictions like these that mess with our vibration and send crazy, push-pull signals rippling throughout the cosmic web. Our orders are received – but they are muddled. Full of negative static and contradictions. With the Universe responding in the same way. We get what we asked for – but it's not what we wanted. So, if you aren't attracting exactly what you want, or keep pulling in repeat experiences with negative outcomes, before you go any further, invest in some deep soul-searching to weed out those ideas or beliefs that are the root cause of this. And replace them with others that support the life you want to live. And that align with the energy of what you want to manifest.

Be kind to yourself during this process. No one can avoid having the odd negative thought. Or even, on occasion, back-sliding into an old mindset. It's your awareness of it that counts. Once you become aware of it, you can acknowledge it and move past it. It's no longer running the show. You've pulled back the curtain and seen the wizard pulling those subconscious levers in your brain. It has no more power over you. And this book will hand you the tools to ensure you keep it powerless – for keeps.

CHAPTER 3

WHAT IS MANIFESTING?

Where did the concept of manifesting come from? The magic of manifesting has been around since the dawn of humanity. Across our most sacred texts, we can find clues that the power of manifesting is ancient wisdom. For example, the Bible tells us: 'Ask and it shall be given, seek and you shall find,' Buddha is quoted as saying: 'We are what we think. All that we are arises with our thoughts. With our thoughts, we make the world.'

Hermeticism was a brilliant spiritual blueprint for manifesting, an Egyptian philosophy dating back to roughly 100 BCE. It emphasized that the Universe is a mental creation and our minds play a central role in shaping our reality. Practiced from around 300 BCE to 1200 CE, it was the OG of showing us how to create our reality.

The Vedic tradition of ancient India dating back to 1500 BCE reveals the concept of 'sankalpa', which means focused intention to resolve. When we align our intentions, thoughts, energy, and action, we shape our destiny. *The Upanishads* text tells us, 'You are what your deep driving desire is. As your will is, so your deed. As your deed is, so your destiny.'

Most practices are designed to first raise awareness or wake us up to who we are and the power we have, and second to begin to play with reality to become creators.

Over the years, new techniques and beliefs have emerged which have added to our understanding of how manifesting works.

13

Each one of these has something valuable to teach us which we can use to superboost our manifesting path. And manifesting itself encompasses several integrated themes:

Law of Attraction – attract by changing your vibration
Law of Assumption – manifesting by assuming it has happened
Cosmic Ordering – place your order directly to the Universe
Quantum Creating – mirroring scientific truths to attract
Manifesting – a blanket term to create your desires.

Hermeticism

There are seven principles of Hermeticism, including the most famous (obviously a successful meme as it lives on all these years later) and one used by astrologers: 'As above, so below.'

Hermeticism tells us that we create what we believe. Our mind creates our reality. That the laws governing the vast Universe also operate within us. Our inner transformation leads to outer results. By aligning our thoughts and beliefs with our desires, we can actively manifest those desires into our lives. When we believe something is possible it manifests and *'The All is Mind; the Universe is Mental'*.

At the heart of Hermeticism is the key principle of vibration: 'Nothing rests; everything moves; everything vibrates.' When we change our vibration, we draw different experiences. Our thoughts and emotions carry a unique energy. By cultivating higher vibrations – through positive beliefs, gratitude, and visualization – we change our resonance and attract experiences that match our desires.

The Law of Attraction is based on the understanding that, at a quantum level, everything in the Universe from the past, the present, and even the future is connected. The energies that we give off vibrate at different frequencies that attract other like energies. Once we understand this, we can use it to our advantage. So, for example, if you're single and you want to draw in the right relationship for you, you have to vibrate at the level you would if that person was already with you and at a similar or the same frequency as them. It also means that if lots of things keep showing up in your life that you don't want, you need to work to change your vibration so it matches what you want to attract.

Here are some of the most important works on manifesting which have contributed to where we are today. We begin with *Thought Vibration: The Law of Attraction in the Thought World* by William Walker Atkinson, published in 1908. This is where the Law of Attraction was first mentioned and elements of this book are still woven into most manifesting practices. Walker Atkinson expressed that thoughts are things that can attract to us what we want. That our mind is a magnet that can attract or repel with the power of our thoughts. He was potentially the first person to come up with the idea of using affirmations. Cutting out fear and worry is a shortcut to increasing your ability to attract what you want, that like attracts like.

This was followed in 1944 by one of the most influential books on manifesting ever written: *Feeling is the Secret* by Neville Lancelot Goddard. In it, Goddard clearly lays out how to create our future and his belief that our imagination was God. And as such, we can imagine and create our future.

Goddard published his book when the most terrible conflict in all of human history was drawing to a close. Millions of people were dead. Millions more wounded, displaced, and traumatized. People needed hope for their future. And also needed the knowledge that no matter their circumstances, they could change them. The world was ready. And one of the most powerful techniques he revealed in his book was the Law of Assumption. That what we assume to be true becomes reality. It is deceptively simple. And also hard to grasp at the same time. Because the truth is, manifesting is as easy as it is difficult. 'Assuming' that we will and do have a great relationship, security, and abundance is an essential key to creating it. To do this, we must truly believe it is possible and act as if we already have it. And there is the rub, moving from a space of doubt to a space of KNOWING and trust. Today, Goddard's teachings are once again gaining popularity in the manifesting community because they are a fast hack to drawing to us what we desire.

Cosmic Ordering is linked to the Law of Assumption. It's the next step in our understanding of how manifestation works. It is based on the principle that the Universe is on your side and the practice of 'ask, believe, and receive'. All you need to do is get really clear on what you want, place your cosmic order to the Universe, and trust that it is on its way – while showing genuine gratitude and giving something back. I've been successfully Cosmic Ordering for years and in 2003 created a DVD guide on how to make it work for you. This has been one of the foundation stones for the steps in this book. One I have expanded on and amplified since, and from which I developed **Quantum Creating**.

Since the 1980s and the explosion of interest in spirituality and self-help, we've also seen an equal and exponential growth in the area of manifestation, fueled in turn by the internet and social media, Abraham-Hicks, *The Secret*, Cosmic Ordering, and my own Quantum Creating. And in recent years the explosion of resources available to us on popular social media platforms. Seeing as all of them have something to teach us and add to the vast resource of manifestation knowledge and techniques available to us, again we're back to that old conundrum: if manifesting is supposed to be so easy, why are my dreams proving so elusive? Which is where this book comes in. So, don't worry. We're going to fix that.

It Begins Within

Nearly all forms of ancient wisdom and esoteric teachings suggest that everything that shows up in our lives is a mirror of our inner world. Advances in science, and in particular in quantum physics, have merged with these teachings, revealing the border where science and mysticism meet. In turn, this has given us a new framework to help us understand the science behind the magic. All you need to know is that everything in the cosmos vibrates with its own particular energy frequency, and everything is connected in the quantum field, including magnificent you!

This means that there is no separation between you and what you want. It already exists and you are already connected to it. To attract what you want, you just have to set your intention and match your vibration to whatever it is you want to draw in, be it a loving relationship, more abundance, or anything else. And, of course, take steps to do the work.

Because manifestation is based on this principle of vibration – which is energy, to put it another way – it's important to realize that the current is always working. It's not something you switch on and off like a light. So, when we talk about working with it, what we mean is getting clear about what you want and clearing away anything that stops the free flow of that current.

Understand that you can do this work at any time. Your future is not set in stone. You are the magician in your own life, and you have the power to create it or direct how it unfolds from here. Change your energy, you change what you attract. And you change your future. However, you don't need to get hung up on how it is going to happen. What matters is the outcome. And as we discussed earlier, it all resides with your assumption that it *will* happen. So, use your energy to visualize the future and KNOW it can manifest as you intend – or most importantly, even better!

For instance, when I was a single parent living in a council flat, I ordered a trip to Tobago, even though there was no way in logical terms I could afford to go to such a place at the time. Even I was surprised at how quickly this arrived as within two weeks I was on a beach on the Caribbean island, drinking rum punch, staring at the turquoise waters of Pigeon Point, with all expenses paid! I had placed my order. I did not spend a moment worrying about how this could happen, I just assumed that it would. The how and the why of it I left to the Universe. Then a friend won a competition at work for selling the most cans of a well-known brand of soft drink. She won a trip to Egypt. But I said I didn't order Egypt – I ordered

Tobago. So she phoned and asked if they could change it – and they did! I have many more examples like this to share with you throughout this book. But for now, I want to reassure you that manifesting can be easy. It really is very simple. The key is to simply get into the flow.

Have Fun With It and Find Your Own Way

Yes, you have to be seriously committed to manifesting what you want. And you have to really, really want it. But that doesn't mean that manifesting is always a serious business. You are allowed to have fun while doing it. In fact, I would say that fun is the secret pinch of love that powers your process.

I was lucky enough to believe in magic and manifesting from a young age. Even when I was broke and struggling and living in my council flat, I never stopped believing in magic. After all, it had worked for me, albeit on an ad hoc basis. During this time, I played with all sorts of techniques to manifest – from lighting and anointing candles to lying on the floor in a circle of clear quartz, clutching two single points in both hands and using them as joysticks to guide me around the cosmos and draw me toward my dreams. I did vision boards, drumming, and anything I felt would help empower my belief and trust that what I desired would come to me.

Disney's *Dumbo* is all about a cute young elephant with over-sized ears. Dumbo is given a feather by his friend, Timothy Q. Mouse. Timothy convinces Dumbo that the feather is magical and gives him the ability to fly. In reality, the feather has no magical powers, but believing in its magic boosts Dumbo's confidence and allows him to soar through the air.

Many of the techniques we can use to superboost our manifesting are our very own magic feathers. We don't need them as the magic is within us all along, but they allow us to 'get out of the way' – or often, get out of our own way. Dumbo let go of the limiting belief that his ears were a problem and in the end that allowed him to fly. It was also Dumbo's belief in magic that gave him the ability to soar. The power is within us all along.

Like all great secret truths, manifesting is essentially easy. It's meant to be accessible and available to all. You already have what it takes to get what you want. There's no special skill set or qualification required of you. I've broken down all you need to know into seven simple steps. And if you follow them and set your intentions, you are in with a good chance of transforming your present and also your future.

The first time you work through this book, please follow the steps in the order they are given. There's a reason for this. Each step builds on the one before it. So, you gain mastery as you go. You've signed up for the gym of the soul. Where we work out your personal program that is designed specifically to get you fit to receive. Once we know how, driving a car is easy. But you wouldn't suggest a learner driver get behind the wheel of a Ferrari. Well, the seven steps are a lot like that. Once you know how to drive, you can operate any car. So, after you have familiarized yourself with the steps, you can then choose to do them in any order you want. Or cherry-pick one or two when you feel you need that extra goal boost to keep you on track.

After experiencing many hilarious, disastrous, and also incredible manifesting miracles, I want to share with you the simplest, most effective methods to clear out any obstacles and hand you the real secrets behind manifesting. Completing and understanding the steps one at a time and in order, the first time around should turbo-charge you, remove blocks, and give you the skills you need to step into your manifesting Ferrari, fast-tracking you to the wonder you deserve.

PART 2
THE STEPS

'A journey of a thousand miles begins with a single step.'
Lao Tzu, Tao Te Ching

And we have not one but seven to take you anywhere on your manifesting adventure that you want to go! But don't worry. I promise that if you follow them, they'll not only get you to the destination where your dreams turn into reality but you're going to enjoy the journey there so much it will seem like a goal in itself.

Step One Unleash Your Unique Soul
Step Two Believe It Is Possible and Know You Deserve It
Step Three Write Your Manifesting Manifesto
Step Four Order with the Joy and Expectation of a Child
Step Five Connect With Your Future Self
Step Six Embrace Co-Creation Power
Step Seven Light Your Soul Lamp

Within each of the step chapters, you'll discover quick and simple Action Steps which will turbo boost your progress. Let's get manifesting NOW!

STEP ONE

UNLEASH YOUR UNIQUE SOUL

Let's talk about unique and unrepeatable you. Because our very uniqueness is a part of our power to manifest. It's the creator within that allows us to form our reality.

You are unique. No one can take your place in the Universe. No one has what you have. Your power is more infinite than you could possibly know. Your uniqueness is your hidden asset to instant manifesting.

We are here to create. To manifest our desires not only to grow our soul but to add to the whole. Our very uniqueness makes us an important piece of the vast machine that is the cosmos.

Without you, the whole world would be different. Strings of coincidences would not happen, without you, a hundred thousand lives would change, and you don't even know it. Your unique energy bouncing around this planet creates ripples of energetic vibration which permeate out to reach others. And like a sacred dance, each action has a reaction. Your energy affects everything.

Every person you meet is like an unwrapped present, they will reveal something new and previously unknown to gift you. Sometimes they just brush past. Other times, they linger. Some people's actions or energy may appear to touch you more than others, but even the small stuff we have no clue about leaps from one person to the next. With one reaction from you, you have inadvertently created a chain reaction of events. This is how powerful you are.

Even if you do nothing at all, you can leap into another energy – someone can see you walking down the street and you mirror something to them. It may be confidence, it may be sadness, but seeing you can trigger something within them that could lead to a major transformation and you know nothing about it.

No matter how weak you feel you are, the truth is how scary your power (and not your powerlessness!) is. Once you understand that you have the key to tapping into it and creating ripples and waves that go your way, you surf the energy of the whole to lead you and, in some ways, us all in a new direction.

We are not separate from each other but particles of energy which collide and affect each piece of solid matter that they hit. Your energy infects everything one way or another.

Following your uniqueness means building a solid relationship with yourself while understanding that all you do affects the whole. Understanding yourself and getting to know you on the most intimate level does not translate into being selfish. Your soul is on a mission and a very important journey. You might not think that your life has been extraordinary – but it is. It is inconceivable that it is any other way. For you are as sacred as any other spirit. And as important. What you have created is what makes all of life possible.

To be able to truly find happiness, you have to face you and form a relationship with yourself that you have always dreamed of. We are hard-wired to crave love externally and seek out our soulmate. But the magic is that our soulmate is within us. And when we understand that, it can then be so much easier to create it from 'outside'. Only then can you have that magical dance with another as well as draw the love from the whole and give it back joyfully and freely. The power of this cannot be underestimated: this can change your life, and in turn the lives of others.

So, what does this mean? You think you know yourself pretty well? Who are you? What have you got to share? How do you feel about yourself? Do you love yourself like a mother loves a child? Do you love yourself the way you would like 'God' or the Universe to love you? Do you love yourself as much as you would expect your ideal lover to love you?

Once you start to form a relationship with yourself, things get exciting and everything changes. The basis of this relationship has to be honesty, understanding, and above all acceptance of all facets of you. Once you start to dig you might find that there are far more levels and parts than you were conscious of. Parts of your personality which have formed to make you safe in all circumstances.

Italian psychologist Roberto Assagioli calls these 'subpersonalities' – different parts of you with their own character which interact with different people or when you are in different moods. I would call it nuances of your soul. Some of these traces can even have been carried over from past lives. You might find that your energy changes when you are around certain people, or your sense of danger is stirred. Often we ignore these feelings. Or we may simply be unaware of them. For instance, are you very different in the way you relate in front of your family, lover, and best friends? If you watch yourself and observe yourself in all situations, you might find that even your voice or your accent changes with different people. We are far more complex than we appear at first glance. Often we ignore these subtle differences that come out with different people and in different circumstances.

Once you start to observe yourself you are likely to find it quite astonishing how many unconscious aspects of you there are. Initially, it might be quite hard not to judge yourself. Later I'll be sharing tips with you to enable you to silence your inner critic or re-record those internal messages you play to flip the dialogue from negative to positive. And to enable you to form the most beautiful friendship and love with yourself. To truly create an intimate relationship with you that lasts a lifetime.

You might say that you have had a hard life, that you have been betrayed, that life has dealt you a terrible hand, and that friends and lovers have let you down. But who has betrayed you the most? Where were you when you needed you the most? Where were you when you made choices to have relationships with people who continually let you down? Who could have saved you and reassured you? The answer is: you could have. Where were you when you needed saving and where were you when you needed strength?

Once you forgive, love, and nurture yourself, everything changes; it cannot not change. You show up for you. You are assured of a different life. You are assured of magic and stepping into a different dimension. You are giving yourself hope and you are assuring yourself that this time it will be different, and it will be different because this time you have you. Once you have you, you have room to love the whole world. You cannot not, for once you grasp your divine power you become aware that you are part of everyone and everything.

Are you expected to be perfect? No. This is about acceptance and, if needed – self-forgiveness. You are asked to have the deepest compassion for yourself. It has been a long journey and to love yourself unconditionally means not just being honest with yourself but also loving yourself through times when you cock things up, when you repeat patterns, and when you do things of which you are not proud or which do not serve your greater purpose.

Once you establish how wonderful and essential it is for you to support you, you can discover another ultimate truth: the Universe loves you. You can rebuild your relationship with the divine. Which simply wants you to understand that you are infinitely loved. The Universe is ALWAYS around you, cheering you on. Through this self-love comes connection and through connection we are able to bring our dreams into reality.

Know Thyself

To know yourself is to love yourself. And if we want to transform our reality, the very first place we begin is within. As well as your internal dialogue, your relationship to yourself is fundamental to your external experience. At the entrance to the temple of the Oracle of Delphi in ancient Greece, circa sixth century BCE, only two words were inscribed: KNOW THYSELF. Often the greatest mysteries – and also the answers to them – are found in full view.

You might think you already know yourself pretty well. So, take a few moments to write down WHO YOU ARE. Because like everything else, your beliefs define this. Right now, write down 20 unique things that make you, you. Is this easy for you? Or are you finding that who you are is something very difficult to pin down? Do you have a strong and unshakable sense of your identity? Or have you lost sight of your unique essence?

29

From a neurological perspective, our mind is filled with neural pathways. These are the support structure of our beliefs that have been ingrained into our being over and over again. And which make up our sense of self-identity. Some of these pathways come from other people. Perhaps someone in your childhood told you over and over that you were stupid? Or you had to act a certain way to win their love and approval?

What we were told may not have been true. But our brains did not know that. And our younger selves were desperate to be loved and accepted. So, our minds soaked up all these untruths. We believed we were unlovable the way we were. Then as adults, we inadvertently continue to feed them. By repeating to ourselves that we are failures. Or that if we express how we truly feel we will be rejected. So we stick to a behavior that seems wrong but we've been told is right. Unknowingly reinforcing those negative neural pathways and losing all sense of our real identity in the process.

Neural pathways are like an information superhighway in our brain. Think of it as a series of interconnected nerve cells, or neurons, that work together to transmit signals. These pathways allow information to travel from one part of the brain to another, or from the brain to the rest of the body. It's like a network of roads for electrical signals in the brain, helping different regions coordinate and carry out various functions, such as thinking, moving, and feeling. They are how our mind stores information.

When we have a new thought, the road is like a tiny dirt track. But the more we repeat an idea or belief, the stronger and wider the roadway becomes until it's as broad as a five-lane freeway. The idea becomes embedded into our brains to the point where we don't even have to think about it – it's automatic. For instance, have you ever driven home on your normal route and found that you don't remember half of it? Evolution knew what it was doing as our brain could not possibly store all these random ideas. However, when we have embedded negative beliefs, not only can they be buried, they can also have an unconscious impact on our daily lives. Hence the importance of really knowing ourselves.

Because it is only when we know who we really are that we can determine what we really want. And what is right for us. Until we understand this, we have all the power of our mind at our disposal but no way to manifest what we need. Which is one more reason why so many of us get mixed results. So, now you see how important it is to be able to define yourself with clarity and not negative criticism.

The magical key to unlock who you really are and set them magnificently free is to look at your thoughts in the moment. Meditation has proven to change the way our brain is formed and can do incredible things for us, from lowering blood pressure to reducing panic attacks, to boosting our creativity and wellbeing, and healing past traumas. When we meditate, we ignore all incoming thoughts and watch them float by us unaffected. We bypass the static and negative dialogue in our heads and instead enter a state of deep inner peace. For you to awaken to who you are, it is essential to become aware of and also to lead your inner voice. We all sometimes have an inner saboteur that either needs to be silenced or, in fact, healed. It too is hurting.

When we begin to challenge this voice, at first it can feel as if it will never change. That the voice can never be silenced. Or

31

even muted. But what you need to remember is that voice is YOURS. It is not an external source with more wisdom than you. On the contrary, you have more wisdom than that voice ever will. It is purely an internalized projection of our fears, our wounds, and our insecurities. Part of changing your energy involves changing your relationship to this voice. If the voice is yours, then surely it deserves love and compassion too? You no longer have to listen to it. But you can now dialogue with it. It has, in fact, been trying to protect you. Even if it has done a painful and terrible job up until now. It has been fed a diet of lies. And you have played a role in continuing to feed it.

So, when you hear that old, negative, and now very tired mix tape start up again – the one which says you're not good enough and are destined to fail – choose to change the conversation rather than trying to silence it. Tell it that you now see that it thought it had your best interests at heart but that both of you have been fed false information and untruths. Which is why, from this point on, you will be speaking only the truth between the two of you. Yes, it may take a while to overwrite the program that has been repeating up until now. But if you can mindfully direct it, you will be well on your way to changing that conversation forever. And changing your energy as you do.

When we are a true expression of our unique and authentic self, manifesting is so much easier. Find the parts of yourself that you feel are unique to you, from your thoughts, dress, hobbies, and imaginings. Build on your uniqueness and joy will follow.

When we tap into our uniqueness, the magic is so much easier. Even from a human success level, taking a good idea and doing it differently with a unique spin can create incredible results. Richard Branson had a vision for discount and mail-order record stores before going on to redefine travel with Virgin Atlantic. Oprah changed the world and became a billionaire bringing a unique spin on the tired old chat-show format. She added real depth and her unique voice. When we have the courage to express ourselves authentically, things fall into place.

Manifesting responds to our unique calls to create a life with difference. What can you manifest that represents the deepest core of you? Here's where your first Action Step comes in to help you manifest only what aligns to your unique self. So, you begin working with yourself instead of against your unrepeatable nature.

ACTION STEP

What Matters to Me the Most?

Here's a secret. Your values define who you are. They reveal what's in your heart and the real you on an integrated, soul level.

When we are young, we are totally clear on what really matters to us. What's precious forms part of an unshakable authenticity around who we are. Yes, of course, our values may change and get upgraded. But more often, we are made to feel we should trade what's priceless and unique to us for what society or other people tell us is valuable. We set off to attain these things – and then wonder why, when we get them, we feel empty, dissatisfied, and unhappy. So we aim for something else. With the same result. And so on in the 'Keeping up with the Joneses' competition for stuff and status.

Don't get me wrong. Wonderful, glorious, good things of life and symbols of success – that dream home or job, the sensual satisfaction of having nice possessions: there's nothing wrong with wanting these things. And for most of us, they form part of what we hope to manifest. But see these as the icing on your cake, not the cake itself, which, like you, is multilayered and uniquely flavored.

The values your unique soul holds as priceless and not for sale, however, usually have very little to do with any of the above. And by reconnecting to them, you get a very clear picture of who you really are. Unique and unfiltered. Not only that, you are then able to manifest what you want so much more easily. Because it is aligned with your true values.

Right now, without over-thinking it, list the five things in your life that you value the most. Just five. Most people can do this really quickly. The faster it flows, the more you are now remembering what really matters – and who you really and uniquely are. Almost always relationships and the people they love will be #1. Then you'll get things like home and security. Then you'll get the intangible stuff like time, health, etc. But these will be slightly different for each and every one of us. Simply because we are all unique.

Now you have them, you can ensure they are arranged in order of importance. Although most come through in exactly that order. Anything else is fine tuning.

Now, not only does this tell you the values that define you, they act as a manifestation checklist you can always refer back to. Say, for instance, someone states that family and relationships are value #1 and the time to spend with them is #2. But they want to manifest a promotion. Now they have created a conflict. A promotion means less time with loved ones, even if it, say, meets value #3, security, as more money from a better-paying job gives that. So, ask the Universe for the promotion, secure in the knowledge that the way this shows up will provide the key to still being able to spend time and nurture your relationships. By doing this you release any part of you that is blocking having a promotion as you fear not spending enough time with your family.

ACTION STEP

Silence the Frenemy Within

To succeed in manifesting, it is ESSENTIAL to have a loving and kind inner voice that wants the very best for you and who KNOWS you deserve it and can do it.

Let's address our inner voice. It broadcasts 24/7. And whether we realize it or not, it is the key to our happiness or unhappiness. Is yours a benevolent spirit guide who supports and loves you? Who guides you toward your best decisions and acts as your inner support network? Or is it that frenemy or a downright persecutor? Are you your own worst critic? Do you say things to yourself you would never say to a friend or anyone you cared about? Getting to know your inner voice and transforming your relationship with it is one of the most profound and simple ways to transform your reality. Because it is this voice that has the most say in what we believe is our reality.

The voice in our head can be a shadowy, fanged version of ourselves. Or our very own best friend, who is filled with wisdom. Trouble is, most of us feed or give in to this inner foe. Our negative self-image, our insecurities, and our fears. The more we feed them, the stronger they grow, drowning out any glimmer of optimism and positivity. Until all we have left is its worries and negativity – which we now mistake for our own.

Their echo is untrustworthy as they amplify all our fears: 'I am unlovable', 'I will never succeed so why bother trying?', and 'People can't be trusted'. The vampire frenemy is only concerned with its own survival. So, it has an ever-evolving box of tricks to stop you from replacing their negative spin.

The good news is, it is an ILLUSION and we have control to transform that destructive voice. Because if you stop listening and instead choose to have faith in yourself, it dies. If you challenge it, however, and shine a light onto whether or not what it is saying is actually true, it shrivels like Dracula in the sunlight. So, time to turf it out of that coffin and drive a stake through that negativity. Reclaim your mind as your own. And know it is the most powerful tool you possess to bring you your desires.

ACTION STEP

Breaking Patterns

Are you ready for an 'Ah-ha!' moment? A pivotal insight that hands you that 'Now I see it!' revelation. One that busts you free of what holds you back? To break a pattern that imprisons us we first need to identify it. And that's what this Action Step is designed to do.

Breaking patterns is the number one key to making space for our manifesting to come in. Begin by looking back over your life fearlessly. What is the most obvious pattern? Have you always been great at earning money but not at finding love? Are you always falling for people who are unavailable? Do you self-sabotage when you reach a goal? Do drama and crisis follow you? Hone down the big ones first, the one or two that seem to have been sticking to you and which you are unable to ditch.

Once you see the pattern, you are in a position to overcome it. Later in this book I will talk about how neural pathways form – often early in life. And how these can crystallize and form negative repeat cycles in our brain. Your ideas or what you have been force-fed to believe, or something repeated, form ingrained beliefs that impact your identity. An interaction at school, your parents' disapproval – if repeated often enough or is traumatic – becomes our reality. Because our brain now sees this as 'normal', we continue to find ourselves in situations that mirror these.

The good news is that we are in a time of awakening and can finally challenge and transform these experiences. And this is one of the main aims of this book. Yes, people repeat the same patterns, particularly in relationships or friendships. Or even with money. The only thing we can change is how we respond to these things.

Think of this as if you are an actor stepping into a long-running role in a Broadway show. Yes, the actors before you had a particular interpretation for the character you are playing. But you want to approach the character in a new way. Your life experience is what draws this out. You ask: What if? How would the audience see this character if you put a different spin on them? The play stays the same. And so does the rest of the cast. But your spin is what makes all the difference. You may create sympathy for the enemy. Or bring shade and nuance into the hero. The audience now sees this character in a new light. And reacts accordingly.

Take a moment to sit quietly and scan all your past relationships. What do they have in common? How do they make you feel? If you look at them from a distance, is there a similar storyline running through all of them? If your relationships were a film, what genre would they be? Thriller? Comedy? Drama? Adventure? Fantasy? What is the story outline?

Is the script about unrequited love? Does the leading actor (you) always fall for untrustworthy partners? Have great lovers but little commitment? Do you go from tough times to riches and then back to struggle again? What do you think is the ending for this story or chapter in your life?

The liberating truth is that you are writing the script and you have control over the storyline. As you rewrite your internal dialogue and transform your neural pathways, thoughts, and beliefs, you create a different outcome.

So, seeing yourself as, yes, yourself, but from this point onwards bringing a new element into your 'performance' results in a different reaction from your 'audience'. And in the case of a recurring one of negative critics, replaces these with positive ones. You break the pattern. Sometimes it's handy to talk to a good friend about what they think our pattern is, as it can be incredibly hard to be objective. Especially if we've been so typecast in one role all this time, we no longer see others available to use. We are the actors and the directors of our life's production. Gaining feedback from our audience, even if it's just an audience of one close friend, can enable us to access so many more ways to remain authentically ourselves, but convey this more powerfully.

These Action Steps peel back the layers of inauthentic habits and thinking that we've camouflaged our true selves with, often as protection and in order to simply survive. Being authentic takes enormous courage on our part as we live in a world where we're placed under so much pressure to conform. Or made to feel we have to be a certain way in order to gain acceptance and love. But paradoxically, this often gets between us and the connection we desire. We serve a filtered 'version' of who we are. And on a subconscious level, others pick that up. Because we are not able to be our true, authentic selves, we attract others who sadly feel they need to do the same. And as neither party feels able to show their true selves, these relationships flounder.

If we don't know who we are, we are unable to manifest what's truly right for us. But you're on your way now. Welcome to the real you.

SUMMARY

Step One
Unleash Your Unique Soul

- Own your unique spirit. Your own journey and voice are important. To expand, to evolve, and to manifest your reality, it's important to have a strong inner voice. To know yourself so you remain aware if others are influencing you against your soul's calling. Embrace your unique voice. Build on all the unique things about you and express them openly.
- Don't bend yourself out of shape to 'fit in'. Embracing your unique soul means knowing that you need do nothing but be authentic. Sure, some connections may fall by the wayside, but they will quickly be replaced by those for whom you don't have to change a thing. And those who love you for every individual quirk and nuance that you have.
- Work on your relationship with yourself: it's the only one you're in that lasts a lifetime. Give yourself the understanding, love, acceptance, and support you seek from your outer connections first. Especially if better relationships are on your manifesting list. Because all change begins with you.
- Rewire your brain for authenticity. Don't continue to buy into the fears, limitations, or even the desire to protect you that you've uploaded from others. Like a virus that infects your system, these keep you stuck, confined, and

40

disconnected from your power. When you hear that old tape begin to run again, thank it, but then consciously choose to overwrite it with the only truth that matters – yours.

- 'Know Thyself'. Imagine these words carved above the entrance to the temple of your soul. Sacred and divine, they remind you that the ultimate key to getting what you want is to embrace your truth. And your magnificence. By understanding yourself and what meets your needs, you automatically set yourself up to receive what is perfectly designed for you.
- Silence the frenemy within. Negative self-talk not only undermines us, it actively disempowers our manifesting brilliance. Its presence in our minds is so insidious, we may be unaware of just how it can influence us. Becoming conscious of our internal dialogue and making the choice to no longer talk about ourselves in a way we would never do about others means we are able to silence the frenemy within.
- Re-record that internal mix tape. Is that ambient thought track positive? Or is it on a loop of negativity? Time to Spotify it more positively to create an anthem of authenticity.
- Break the pattern. Identify those recurring themes or old storylines that keep you stuck, or simply manifesting the same old outcomes. Know you can change this at any time simply by consciously making a different choice or even how you react. You are not just the star of your own story but the writer, producer, and director as well. YOU decide the theme from this point onward. And the ending. Find those patterns that trip you up. Once you see them, you can break free of them. The past does not define you.

STEP TWO

BELIEVE IT IS POSSIBLE AND KNOW YOU DESERVE IT

Now you've revealed the magnificence of who you really are in Step One, you're pumped and primed for the next step: where you embrace possibilities and deservedness so that the real magic can begin!

As basic as it sounds, knowing it is possible for you to have whatever it is you want to manifest is an essential step to making it happen. If we don't truly believe it is possible, it is unlikely to happen. Honing this belief leads to a clear pathway of success. It's the very foundation of attraction and the building blocks of manifestation. Which is why it's important to begin with expanding what you believe is possible.

Sounds simple, right? Believe that it IS possible. I cannot tell you how crucial the first part of Step Two is. Our beliefs are deeply ingrained. If you have never experienced what you desire, there might be a part of you, a tiny inner voice that is trained to protect you. An underground cynic that is worried that if you don't get your manifestation, you will be gutted. Or perhaps it is an old loop of fear from situations that never worked out. Nailing this step opens a gateway to delivery.

Chances are that whatever specific thing you want to manifest, there might be an unconscious belief that it isn't possible for you, which creates a block to it having happened. It's super-important to dig down and find the weeds that are covering the truth, to pluck out those false beliefs like 'I am not lovable' or 'I will never have money'. Tackling that, diving into and facing your fear, challenging those sticky beliefs and moving into a space where you KNOW you are certain you can manifest, gives you a magical key to make it happen. Here's an example.

I am experienced in manifesting and understand it left, right, and center. Yet I spent decades not being able to manifest the relationship I wanted. Yes, I had romance, lust, and even commitment. But in all those relationships I never trusted that I was truly loved. Because I never believed it, I ended up manifesting only half of what I asked for and dealt with many struggles within those relationships.

Because of my neglect and loneliness as a child, I had a hardcore superhighway neural pathway, which was creating real problems for me. I had an intense belief in love and was a true romantic at heart. I have five planets in Pisces – including Venus, the planet of love and abundance, in the most romantic sign. So while I believed in love and was always optimistic that I would experience the kind of love I imagined, I didn't realize that the extent of my unconscious conviction that I was unlovable was sabotaging me from manifesting this.

Why? This was my deepest childhood wound and the hardest belief to shift.

I gravitated toward relationships where I was the giver, the rescuer, and swept in like the proverbial knight in shining armor. Because of my past and my undiagnosed ADHD, I found it very hard to regulate my emotions. And this set me up for constant heartache.

44

So what changed? How did I find an equal, divine partner to dance through life with? After trying for years to make work a committed relationship that was dramatically failing, I got to the point where I had reached my limit. Suddenly I knew with all of my being that I was worth more than this. That I was worthy of love and that love could and would be drawn to me.

There was a fundamental change within me. I had spent several months in therapy and, step by step, I believed I was worthy of love. It was like a switch had been flipped. Finally – I knew I deserved it.

My then-partner and I decided to amicably divorce and I went to London to see a divorce lawyer. I felt free for the first time in many years and I had a true sense that the next chapter was going to be different. I wasn't focusing on future relationships, and in fact, I was looking forward to being single. Yet at the same time, I truly, wholeheartedly believed that it was not only possible but that love and a different experience would find me when the time was right. I felt comfortable in my own skin and excited about the next chapter. I was looking forward to exploring life and being free to do as I pleased.

I live in Devon, so I always love to catch up with my friends when I'm in town. I met up for lunch with an old friend, Jane, who used to be a TV executive commissioning programs for television. During that lunch I asked Jane if she could suggest a filmmaker as I had been consciously manifesting one to work with and I figured she might know one near me. Always, when manifesting, be practical as well as expecting it to be delivered! Do the work. And work your group – which I'll talk about in Step Six.

Jane replied that actually she did know someone who was currently taking a break from television. The woman was an award-winning director who made stunning films which looked more like water color paintings than TV. She mentioned that we were meant to meet at her wedding, but neither of us could attend (wrong timing!). And she always wondered how we would get on as we were both creative in our own ways as well as being feisty and, in her words, 'fabulous'.

Intrigued, I wrote to Cathy and asked if she would be interested in meeting me to discuss freelance work. Cathy, as it turned out, lived 25 minutes up the road from me (I live in the middle of nowhere) and we arranged to meet a couple of days later. I didn't think much of it. However, when I opened the door to Cathy and our eyes met, we both paused for a moment. I was so disconcerted that I turned away. And instead of inviting her in for a cup of tea, I turned left, so my back was to her, and gave her a tour of the castle. I had this overwhelming sense of knowing.

I felt flustered as there was a mutual recognition. When we came downstairs and had our meeting, we were mesmerized by each other. Not only had I manifested a film maker – but also a wife! Cathy lives her dream of filming nature and traveling the world and she films all my astrology videos and takes all my photos. Don't get me wrong, like all relationships we had to work hard at it, but the Universe delivered.

The key was, it wasn't until I knew I was lovable (we all are!) and believed it was possible that I met my equal partner, wife, and inspiration. My relationship with Cathy at the time of writing is eleven years old and growing, evolving, and the greatest blessing.

Cleansing Our Energy From the Not Possible

Our surroundings and culture hold significant sway over the stories we spin about ourselves, molding the myths we buy into about what we can achieve. Think of these tales as stories – little nuggets of narrative passed around like wildfire. These stories can be true or false, blurring the lines between reality and perception. If our mind is bombarded with ideas that everyone believes, our brain soaks them up like mice at a cheese convention.

These beliefs are held by us but also, like the current most popular memes, stories, trends, and ideas, shaping our beliefs about our potential long before we even attempt to test them out. And the impact? Well, it can be pretty mind-blowing.

Take, for instance, the time when everyone was dead certain that running a mile in under four minutes was utterly impossible. Then along came Roger Bannister in 1954, a med student who shattered that belief by doing just that. But here's the kicker – his achievement didn't just stop there. Shortly after, someone else pulled off the same feat, and before you knew it, running a sub-four-minute mile became the new norm. Suddenly we have a new reality and a lesson on the impact of our beliefs on our achievements.

Similarly, when American educator Jane Elliott decided to give her students a firsthand experience of racism in the aftermath of Martin Luther King Jr.'s assassination in 1968, she never anticipated the ripple effect her experiment would cause. She divided her class into those with brown eyes and those with blue eyes. Elliott made up a pseudo-scientific explanation about how eye color was related to intelligence and the class, divided by eye color, took it in turns to be on 'top'. Not only did the children start to behave differently according to the different story spun about their superiority, but those who were told they weren't as intelligent began to struggle with tasks they had easily handled before.

Although this experiment is controversial by today's standards (we would never subject a child to this kind of experiment) and considered unethical (as the children did not give informed consent before taking part), the results were astounding and show us that we are what we believe and we create what we believe. ESPECIALLY when it comes to our beliefs about ourselves. It demonstrates how it's all too easy to internalize these stories, letting them become woven into the fabric of our reality. And in so doing, limit ourselves (ironically to keep us psychologically safe from disappointment) about what is possible for us.

Transformation begins with challenging the stories we tell ourselves, embracing the boundless potential that lies within each of us, and expanding the parameters of what we truly believe is possible for us.

> 'The happiness of your life depends upon the
> quality of your thoughts.'
> *Marcus Aurelius, Meditations*

If you find that you cannot seem to get beyond repeating certain kinds of patterns and experiences, or that you don't truly believe that it is possible to draw new things into your life, there is a way through!

Advances in fields such as quantum physics have shown us that the Universe is a place of amazing possibility, and we've only just begun to touch the edges of truly understanding its infinite nature. Today, we have a greater understanding of the role that consciousness and our minds play in connecting us to the vastness of what is possible. And how this can help us explore even further the outer limits of our potential.

Consciousness is an awareness of thought that lies beyond thought itself. It's consciousness that allows you to step back from your thoughts and say: What do I think about what I think? And even more powerfully: Would it be better if I thought something different? This is an essential key to manifesting. Because both work on the basis of what we actually think and believe (and not what we know we should think or believe). What we think and believe feeds out into the Universe and acts as an attractor force.

Shamans have been telling us since the dawn of time that if we want our outer world to change, we must transform ourselves. Which, of course, begins with Step One – revealing our unique souls. When we see ourselves differently, we are transformed. We can then effortlessly step into the cosmic web of non-ordinary reality; or what a Shaman might experience as being another layer of a much wider reality. Or even what theoretical physics terms 'the multiverse'.

But here's the thing. It's our mind, with all of its thoughts, that allows us to understand that this is what we need to do. But our mind can only take us so far because of the inevitable limits that exist around our thinking. Our mind can take us to the door that leads us to non-ordinary reality, or the whole of the Universe. But we have to go beyond our mind to fully step through it. Co-creation is most powerful when we do it from the space of non-ordinary reality, or the whole of the cosmic web of infinite possibility that exists in the Universe. That's where futures that our ordinary minds struggle to imagine are found.

When we co-create from just our mind, we are likely to merely recreate a different form of the past rather than a magical, limitless future.

Here's a cheat sheet to ditch the struggle. A humble sandwich might reveal the barriers to your creativity. Yes, a sandwich!

ACTION STEP

Assemble Your Sandwich!

When we know this, everything we think is possible changes. Let's do an experiment. Think of a sandwich, any sandwich: you supply the detail. It's almost one hundred percent certain that the sandwich that sprang to your mind will be a full or composite representation of a sandwich you have previously encountered.

It might be the sandwich you ate for lunch yesterday. Or a picture of a sandwich that you've conjured up after seeing somewhere. But it's highly unlikely you immediately thought of a sandwich that lies beyond your direct or indirect experience. This becomes especially interesting if you are from a culture where sandwiches aren't the norm. If that's the case, your trusty brain will have ferreted around for any images of sandwiches you might have come across in films or adverts, or drawn a total blank.

The point about this tasty exercise is to show you one of the ways in which we know the mind works. The mind is a bit like a computer with an extraordinary filing system that links things in many ways for various useful reasons. As we take in information, it codes and stores it for later retrieval. Imagine that you are watching Netflix and you see a drama about a holiday showing a sandcastle. Now imagine that you have a million tiny librarians on standby in your mind, waiting to help you find references for all of the information you are receiving through all of your senses. As the sandcastle flashes up on Netflix, the librarians will check the information coming in and say: You've seen that before ... Where did I store that image? Ah! Over there in the Childhood Holiday section. That's a sandcastle! Right, but we're adults now and we're not on holiday, we're watching Netflix. Do we have a section called Movies? We do! So, let's put it there. And we'd better create a subsection called Holiday Movies. Then we'll link this to the Childhood Holiday section so we can cross-reference whenever we need to.

This is why learning something totally new takes us a bit longer, because we are having to create the internal infrastructure in which we can store the information. Manifesting a future that matches your desires. But because your mind works by processing information that you already know, it takes a huge leap to get beyond that to what you don't know and can't imagine because you haven't had any direct or indirect experience of it yet. As a result, we can go about the whole co-creation bit by falling back on what we are familiar with rather than generating something truly new and incredible.

This is why we often find ourselves going in circles around the same problems or situations that appear repeatedly in our lives. As Einstein observed: We can't solve problems by using the same kind of thinking we used when we created them.

All in all, this means that we have to be really conscious to stretch beyond the limits of our thinking to get to all the good stuff. But where is it and how do we get there?

Remember, you are already part of the whole, so you are already connected to all that is within the entire Universe – past, present, and future. In order to do it, you have to go beyond the mind. That's why so many ancient religions and magical practices involve meditation or entering trance-like states from which we can access the door that separates the limits of our ordinary mind and step into that non-ordinary reality.

ACTION STEP

Free Your Mind

Let's try it! Get yourself into a place where you won't be interrupted and let yourself daydream. Some of the greatest creative strokes of genius have arrived when people have been staring into the flames of a log fire in a grate, lying in bed just before going to sleep, or musing as they look out of a window.

You really want to follow a feeling and get curious about where it will take you. Let's say you've been trying to attract money because you think it will make you feel safe. The idea of money being the thing that might make you feel safe has probably come from your past experiences – in the same way that the memory of a thousand sandwiches that you've eaten in the past means that the next time you're hungry your helpful mind is likely to say, 'How about a nice sandwich?'

But suppose you start with feeling safe and carry that feeling into the cosmic web. In that case, you may be drawn toward many other things that vibrate with the energy of safety that lie beyond your ordinary imagination. Even if nothing clear comes to mind, you just get a sense of possibility, know that you're onto something big. When it's time to come back to your everyday life, bring back your experience of being in that place of infinite possibility and let that feed into your mind.

See what happens when you work with this process over time. You may find that it begins to change what you intend to attract as you process new information that comes from this place of infinite possibility. You will have a new relationship with what is possible. You load your sandwich with new fillings. Or even start with different bread. By doing this, you get a taste of what is possible. And you may discover that amazing new experiences that taste far better than anything you might have consciously asked for start showing up in your life.

Opening ourselves to new information and experience is the very thing that helps us evolve. As we evolve, we become more powerful creators who can draw on the infinite abundance of the entire Universe in the process of creation itself.

So How to Get There? How to Access the Magical Portal That is KNOW IT IS POSSIBLE?

'Ideas are alive, that ideas do seek the most available human collaborator, that ideas do have a conscious will, that ideas do move from soul to soul, that ideas will always try to seek the swiftest and most efficient conduit to the earth (just as lightning does).'
Elizabeth Gilbert, Big Magic: Creative Living Beyond Fear

We all need inspiration. One of my favorite books that I plunge into when I am stuck in my writing is *Big Magic* by Elizabeth Gilbert. It talks about getting out of the way to let the magic in. That ideas are alive and floating about waiting to enter us and to become 'real'. That great ideas and creative inspiration are otherworldly. And the more an artist allows inspiration to flow through them, trusting the process and opening themselves to it, the greater the ideas and work.

Manifesting is exactly like this. If we live in a place of belief, then what we desire and know is possible (or more) will appear in the most extraordinary ways. It is already out there, a spell waiting to be cast. The world will shift on its axis as suddenly as if it is a world where magic exists.

Many people ask me why it is that I seem to be able to create and manifest things so 'easily'. A dear friend who read tons on manifesting and perfectly understood the concept questioned if it was just a skill I have. Not everyone is an opera singer, for example, they love opera, they sing a little, but she wondered if it was like that, an innate gift.

I can categorically say no. Why has it been easier for me? Because as mentioned, I was lucky enough to live the first step from a very young age. I didn't have the usual conditioning that magic is just fantasy. I had my eyes peeled to see the impossible and then to expand on it.

We all fall prey to confirmation bias. We are unconsciously programmed to seek out and experience what we believe. Confirmation bias is a mental shortcut that can trip us up when we gather information. We're much more likely to believe information confirming our beliefs and downplay or ignore evidence that would prove us wrong.

Let's say there's a politician/actor we don't like. We unconsciously seek out news that portrays them negatively. We fuel our beliefs by avoiding articles that are positive about them. We can even misremember information, as our brain always wants to be proven right.

If something goes wrong for us in the morning and we tell ourselves it's a bad day, we tend to grab any tiny thing that goes wrong to 'prove' our belief and in turn create more problems. (Hint: Always wake up expecting a good day!)

Why do we do this? Our brain is constantly bombarded with information and confirmation bias helps us by being a super-fast filter, taking up much less energy than constantly reevaluating information.

There's a comfort in feeling secure about our preconceived ideas, but a lot of the time it is an illusion or, at the very least, an exaggeration. So, what can we do about it? It's crucial to regularly question our beliefs and take in different points of view.

Confirmation bias influences our lives in such powerful ways. If we meet a friend of a friend that we don't like, we can leap upon any mistake or misstep they make to shore up our opinion. While it's a clever mind trick, it can lead us down the wrong path.

When we start to replot, reroute, and reimagine what we believe is possible, the confirmations will come. Turn your confirmation bias into sniffing out the wonder waiting to come in. You can learn to marvel at the magic in the world, the twists, the turns, the synchronicities. When we believe in the magic with our arms wide open to possibilities and expect the magic to happen, we step into a world that is different, one where successful manifesting becomes a reality.

Shifting to Knowing It Is Possible

If you could manifest only one thing, what would it be? What is your soul's greatest calling? How are you going to make it happen? What does it look like, what makes it the thing you want the most? Do you know? Are you certain that it is possible for you? That manifesting it is your destiny? That when you order it, it will be so?

Step One and its Action Steps, together with examining your beliefs so far in Step Two to shed those negative beliefs, have prepared you for your next action. The more casually, easily, and relaxed you can visualize what you want, the more you open the gateway to it happening.

I read a fabulous article that illustrates this clearly. The stunning actor Barry Keoghan (*Saltburn*) was talking about how he has been manifesting his whole life. He does it in the form of To-Do lists on his phone. Barry was interviewed by *GQ* magazine and said he had written on his To-Do list to be on the cover of *GQ* and that was why he was sitting there now. 'I am not shitting you, I wrote it down,' he told the journalist. 'To call them forth from the Universe.' He has manifested many things with this technique, from being in Hollywood to different directors he wanted to work with.

Barry so effortlessly expresses the secret of 'knowing it is possible', he simply pops into his To-Do list what he knows he could and would achieve.

This is an important reminder. If we order something that we don't believe is possible (I want to order becoming a real-life unicorn), then of course it is not going to happen. So don't order things you know are impossible, and when you are ready to create your reality, deeply examine your beliefs. What wild imagining will you put in your to-do list today?

Ariana Grande tweeted in 2011, 'Loved seeing *Wicked* again ... amazing production! Made me realize again how badly I want 2 play Glinda at some point in my life! #DreamRole.' Her path to manifesting her role in *Wicked* is a masterclass in manifesting! She didn't stop dreaming about it; she even stocked up on pink clothes and wondered what underwear Glinda would wear. Ariana embodied it before it became hers. Five auditions and twelve years later she achieved her dream, belief acting as if it has already happened (Law of Assumption), and practical action!

Knowing You Deserve It

Step Two actually has two parts. First, we looked at our ability to believe in order to receive. But now it's time to move on to the second half of the equation: Deservedness.

Again, on the surface it seems simple. Sure, I deserve it! But do you know you are worthy of love? That you deserve security, abundance. etc.? Hopefully after Step One and doing your Action Steps, you will have surrendered any doubts or unconscious blocks. Knowing we deserve to have what we want is essential for our orders to come in.

ACTION STEP

Turning Drama into Deserving

There's a drama exercise that's great fun to do if you can persuade a group of friends to give it a go. Sit in a circle and pick one word which you will each take in turn to say with a totally different meaning behind it. The rest of the group then guesses the meaning behind your delivery.

Take a simple word like 'Yes'. You can say 'Yes' so that it actually means any of the following: 'No', 'Do I have to?', 'Maybe', 'Who, me?', 'I don't understand', 'I'm not sure', 'I'm not actually listening but I'm saying this to try to get you off my back.'

You can also say it so that it means 'Yes', 'Yes PLEASE', 'Oh how fantastic!', 'Really?' or 'Let's go right now!'

We do this when we are talking with each other all the time – say one thing and mean another, or play with emphasis or even our facial expression to make what we have said mean loads of different things.

It's exactly the same when we work with manifesting. This works on the principle that like attracts like. It says that what

---

58

shows up in our world is a reflection of our vibration, what we believe, and that if we want to change what shows up, we have to change our belief to match the vibration of whatever it is we want.

If you really want to totally grasp what is actually going on, the simplest way is to understand that, no matter what you say, the Universe always gets what you really mean. In other words, the Universe hears your subtext. The Universe knows when you are really saying, 'I want a really great job (but actually, I don't think I'm worth it, so please make sure I don't get one). And by the way, if you think you can push one in my direction, I'll make sure I blow my chances!' It knows when you are saying, 'I deserve to be in a loving, committed relationship (but who could love someone as awful as me?).'

Believe the Unbelievable

Still unsure? Maybe you're thinking that it's all very well to use celebrities as examples of people who have successfully manifested their dreams – but you still retain a core belief that these kinds of things don't happen to 'ordinary' people like you.

If that's the case, let me share Kevin's story with you. Kevin Johnson, 34. A carpenter from East London. Living in a rented flat with his wife Dee and their four kids. In other words, an ordinary, hard-working guy. Like many people, Kevin would dream about owning his own home. Not just any home, however. A luxury home with plenty of space that was big enough for all of them.

Kevin had been entering house raffle competitions online. He never really thought he would win. He was happy to be giving money to charity. But then, something inside him changed. From 'why not me?' to 'well – why NOT me?' He adopted a more positive mindset when a house just 15 minutes from where the family was living was put up for raffle. He cut out a picture of the house from a newspaper and showed it to his son, telling him this would be where they were moving. He would walk past the house and know that they were going to be living there. He even put off paying for a parking permit for his van which was about to run out at his old address because he had a feeling he was going to win. And he did.*

Kevin had been taking the actions necessary to manifest his dream home given his income – i.e., buying a raffle ticket. But his mindset of 'I probably won't win' was getting in the way and sending mixed messages to the Universe. When he changed to a more positive one of 'Well, why shouldn't I win?' and discovered there was no reason why not, he aligned his energy and his actions. So, the Universe was able to deliver. But this tells you that if Kevin can – you can too!

Incidentally, many of these raffle house winners talk of their win as a direct result of their efforts to manifest their dream home. They admit this took some time (and many entries), but also that they did not doubt they would eventually succeed. Their belief that it was possible was unshakable. And they were in no doubt that they deserved it.

* Welch, Andy, 'Too good to be true? What it is really like to win a £3m dream home', *Guardian*, 4 April 2023, https://www.theguardian.com/lifeandstyle/2023/apr/04/too-good-to-be-true-what-it-is-really-like-to-win-a-3m-dream-home

So How Do You Avoid Sending Out Mixed Messages?

1. Understand that you are always in communication with the Universe. If you tell the Universe that you deserve a loving, committed relationship, and then ten minutes later see a couple walking hand in hand and think 'That could never happen to me', you're going to slow down the speed of attraction.
2. Be honest about when you might be giving out mixed messages. Pay attention to any part of you that offers resistance when you talk or think about what you want. It can be as clear as an inner voice telling you good things can never happen to you, or as subtle as the muscles in your shoulders contracting or your tummy turning over in a way that you know isn't excitement.
3. Be kind to yourself. Thinking, 'Oh no, there I go again, I can't do anything right!' when you catch yourself working against yourself puts you in a vibrational state that probably isn't lined up with what you want. Notice it, bless it, and let it go.

ACTION STEP

To Catch a Meme

We've all heard, shared, and enjoyed memes. We pass them on, we relate to them, and they can give us a sense of community. The term 'meme' has a fascinating back story. It was coined by the evolutionary biologist and professional skeptic Richard Dawkins in his book *The Selfish Gene*. In it, he talks about the fact that perhaps we don't just evolve by our genes alone but through our ideas. And that our ideas act like a virus which leaps from brain to brain. And of course, in today's interconnected world, they spread by social media and the internet.

What Dawkins may not have realized is that he was actually talking about the collective unconscious. The fact that we are all, in fact, connected. And this includes our thoughts. When we reach the point where a significant number of us have the same belief in an idea, then we all embrace it or move on, as a whole.

We can see how this has influenced our evolution throughout history. And that human progress is tied to it. And yes, it often means letting go of what we previously believed to be true and replacing this with what is a new, refined idea based on previously unknown facts. Our worldview has changed. And we along with this.

But what does that mean for us as individuals and manifesting magicians? How can we transform our lives and our manifesting skills with this knowledge? The term 'meme' has been hijacked by the internet, but this can be a great analogy. We all want our posts to go viral or receive the most likes or shares. Like a song we hear once on the radio which turns into the earworm you're humming along to, ideas can stick. Our minds are constantly in search of new ones to latch on to. Which is why someone can post their tattoo of a snake on Instagram – and the next minute there are hundreds of thousands of people walking around with snake tattoos, all of them thinking they're original.

I have a tattoo sleeve. Where did I get that idea? Perhaps without realizing it, I was inspired by a meme. This is how we all become infected by ideas that seem like our own and totally original. And how ideas are just like viruses: invisible and easily spread.

Our brains are therefore exactly like computers. We upload ideas like the latest app. They become part of our operating system. And then part of who we believe we are. When we're children, we have cultural ideas programmed into us. Or the ideas of our parents. And these ideas form very specific neural pathways – for good or bad. We may not be aware of just how much they influence us however. Like a program which is constantly running in the background, some of these ideas may boost our performance. If you were lucky enough to have parents who told you that you were smart and capable, and who gave you the opportunity to problem-solve without helicoptering, then you grow up confident in yourself and your abilities.

But for those of us who had a more difficult upbringing, or parents who told them they were stupid or unattractive, these ideas, even if our conscious minds now tell us this is untrue, can continue to overshadow our existence. Because our brains have accepted the original programming and the neural pathways are still active. The good news, however, is that we can reroute or totally rewrite these thanks to something called neuroplasticity.

Imagine your brain as a thought tree. Its branches represent the connections between neurons. As you learn and experience the world, these branches grow and reach out, forming new connections. Some branches will thicken and strengthen with repeated use, while others, if not nurtured and encouraged, might wither. Neuroplasticity is our brain's ability to change shape and structure, adapting to its environment. When we change our brains, we change our lives. The fabulous news is that we can control that.

Troubleshoot Your Way to a Trouble-Free Mindset

Identifying these embedded ideas and the memes we may unconsciously carry around is the key to successful manifesting. Because we are not only dealing with our own thoughts and beliefs, but also those of the whole. Since we are under constant barrage from this, how can we make it work for us? In many ways, what we program into our brain becomes the algorithm that draws to us our experiences. Once we understand the depth of that, we can change it. So, let's sort it out.

One of the hard parts of unpicking our beliefs is that they seem 'normal' to us. For instance, what do you tend to eat for breakfast? You might plump for avocado on toast, porridge, or perhaps a fry-up? We are programmed for a deep-seated response to breakfast. When we leap out of bed in the morning, we have a limited menu. Depending on your life experience it's scrambled eggs or miso soup, Rice Krispies versus stewed black-eyed-pea sandwich. Curry versus kippers. This is just a very small example of how we have embedded beliefs that we take for granted, none of which is 'true' but rather just learned experience.

Let's nail this down to a few simple steps you can take to root out beliefs that no longer serve you. Because like everything about this entire process, it's meant to be easy!

1. **Be vigilant.** When making a decision, or even deciding what you want to manifest, take time out to really weigh up all the facts. Facts, not opinions. If you find yourself

changing your decision because someone else (family/ friends/that group, etc.) disagrees with you or tells you that you can't, remind yourself that you are free to choose. Whenever you feel yourself agreeing with a group, especially if you know it is wrong – or wrong for you – then choose to DISAGREE. Choose your influence. And free yourself to be truly you.

2. **Write it down.** Before you announce what you want to manifest, especially anything that people may disagree with or react negatively to, write it down. Explore it fully. Know why you are doing it and how passionately you feel about it. Find support from others who believe in your power to manifest it. Choose your audience. And only run it by people whose support you can count on.

3. **Stalk your thoughts.** Listen to what you say and think. Your inner voice and intuition will KNOW when you are kidding yourself or agreeing for the sake of it. Pay attention to your feelings, your physical reactions within your body, and note down any discomfort – emotional, mental, or physical. If necessary, take a time out or don't commit – just yet. It may be that your goal is in a state of refinement. Or you have yet to discover what it is you REALLY want.

All these processes remove 'can't' and 'won't' and replace them with 'can' and 'shall'. They shift your beliefs around what you think you deserve to knowing you are deserving. You're now ready for the next step – the most crucial when it comes to making what you want appear. Get ready to create your Manifesting Manifesto!

SUMMARY

Step Two
Believe It Is Possible and Know You Deserve It

- Check your belief system. Are you running those tired old tunes of limitation and lack? Imagine replacing them with new tracks around fresh possibilities. Change that playlist.
- Reach for the stars! Know you are worthy of love and an incredible life.
- Trust that unlimited abundance is available to you.
- Put in your order and believe that your order will arrive. I always describe it as ordering off Amazon – you don't doubt they will deliver or keep checking your order status every two minutes.
- Watch for mixed messages. Yes, you want it. But is that inner saboteur telling you that you'll just f*** it up like you normally do if you get it? That sends a contradictory message to the Universe, which results in you reinforcing your negative belief about yourself. Change the dialogue – change the delivery.
- Hone your focus but don't be too specific. You can't say, for instance, 'I want X to fall in love with me.' But you can say, 'I manifest the perfect love for me right now.'
- Layer that sandwich with a different filling. Don't opt for the familiar or something you've been content with in the past. Does that old ham and cheese really satisfy you? Get a taste for something new. Whatever you can imagine – the Universe contains so many more options. So, visualize your ideal – and also be open to something better.
- Catch a meme: memes can be fun and entertaining. But not if what they spread are messages that discourage or limit our beliefs about what is possible for us. Fact finding

and discovering the truth play a big role in honing the purity of our vision that's necessary for manifesting success. And simply living with joy. So, just because others accept one idea doesn't mean you should – find out for yourself whether it's true for you. Root out these thoughts and question everything.

STEP THREE

WRITE YOUR MANIFESTING MANIFESTO

manifesto \man-uh-FESS-toh\ noun: a written statement
declaring publicly the intentions, motives, or views
of its issuer.

Merriam-Webster

A Manifesting Manifesto is a commitment to ourselves. It lays
down our intentions. It is a document that holds us to account on
our manifesting journey. Our manifesto records what we know
we can create (because we deserve it and know it's possible). It
captures our passion and excitement for the future, which I will
go into in Step Five (Connect with Your Future Self).

Your Manifesting Manifesto is your declaration of power. It's
where you boldly outline your desires and map out your path
to achieving them. This document is your promise to create the
life you deserve.

Within your manifesto, you recognize your limitless potential
and tap into the burning passion that drives you toward an
extraordinary future.

I don't know about you, but there have been times in my life
when I have half-heartedly committed to things that I enjoy and
really want to do – like going to the gym or meaning to walk the
South West Coast Path. Only to put them on the back burner
or be distracted by life. When we write things down, it takes an
idea or a longing and it brings it into the world. We are giving

birth to our intentions. We are saying to our mind and soul that this is important and to turn our energy toward it.

From a technical point of view, our brain has to deal with daily information overload. And we only have limited mental resources to deal with this. Writing superboosts our 'encoding' process where the brain is alerted to the fact that this information is important. It needs to be prioritized and then stored in our long-term memory rather than being shoved in the brain's discard pile so that our subconscious mind can be continually processing it in the background. In other words – it's a system update.

Writing has always been important in the spiritual and magical world. Spells and grimoires, spiritual texts, all capture the secrets through the written word. From the beginning of time, even before the written word, humans have created cave art and god-dess sculptures, amulets for protection and abundance. There has always been a fundamental need to have a tangible expression of what we want to make happen. Jotting things down captures a thought and turns it into a reality. Holding an amulet reminded ancient folk that they were protected. Believing/knowing they were protected was arguably an early form of manifesting.

We are preparing ourselves for success, we acknowledge our magical and practical power to make things happen, to succeed.

How to Write a Manifesting Manifesto to Align Your Energy With Your Desires

It is super-important that you handwrite your manifesto. Numerous studies have shown that when we write things down, we are more likely to achieve them. Handwriting activates

Most of the time, no matter how hairy the deadline or what barriers lay between you and your goal, you achieved it. That's because your entire attention, energy, and resources were focused at that point in time on that one goal. You backed that up with determination and usually the belief that no matter what, you would accomplish that. This is the power of intention.

We've also all heard stories about parents being able to lift cars off their trapped children when normally they would struggle even carrying their child. Again, this is the intention focused during a crisis. But we do not need a crisis to occur to be able to tap into this incredible power that resides within us all. We can all harness this ability simply by shifting our focus onto one major goal we want to achieve. And 'focus' is the key word here. Think about a laser beam. That is concentrated light, right? Ordinary light is diffuse. On a subatomic level, particles of light scatter in all directions and bump around into one another. So, they can even interfere with one another by doing this. A laser, however, aligns all the particles so they are beamed in one direction, layering them upon each other so instead of being scattered and diffuse, the light becomes so powerful it can be channeled to cut through objects. But it is still light.

Now you understand this you can focus all your intention toward one major goal. For a while you are going to have tunnel vision as you bring to it the laser-like attention it deserves. Your heart knows which goal it is, so please listen to it if you have several big goals right now and be guided by your intuition, which is always your best compass.

Now, think back to a time when you focused your intention on something you absolutely, positively had to have or do. As you feel that emotional focus come back to you, now direct it onto this goal and keep it focused there. Know beyond a shadow of a doubt that you have the ability to manifest this goal – just as you manifested whatever it was you were trying to achieve in the past. You already have proof that the process works, but now you are consciously honing and using it.

As the saying goes: where intention goes, energy flows. Focus your attention on your goal and you will begin to see incredible progress toward it as synchronicities and opportunities line up in your laser line of sight. Turn on the power of intention and transform your life.

Your visualizations in the early stages are fragile plants that can easily be stunted or killed if exposed to the wrong elements. The problem with sharing what you want to achieve or allowing others to see what your dreams are is that so many people out there are only too happy to shoot them down or rain on your parade. They may do this because they are scared, because they are jealous, or because they fear that you attaining what you desire will shift the dynamic of your relationship and they may no longer be relevant in your life. They may even want to protect you from disappointment or failure and have the best heartfelt intentions.

All thoughts are energy, and in the beginning you need to keep the energy around your dreams and visualizations close and nurture it in order to manifest them. So, all it may take is a few negative comments or a well-meaning person to start questioning your ability to get what you want and your visualization energy is diminished. This can easily happen when people come into your home and see things like your vision board or you share your goals with them too early. If you keep your goals to yourself but accessible to you and those you trust who are on the same journey, then all that energy goes where it needs to go: straight to your goal.

Evolve Your Goals With Your Soul

There's one more thing you need to do before you add a goal to that brand new sparkling manifesto. That is to check whether it's still truly, madly, deeply what you want.

Before you add that old desire that's been on your To-Make-Real list for however long you've been at this, stop and check whether it is still relevant and also that it complements and is aligned with the rest of the goals on your list. Because unless you do, that old desire or dream could in fact interfere with you attaining that current and better one.

As we evolve and grow, what we want changes with us. Of course, some dreams remain timeless and relevant. However, their form may change. The qualities we may have prioritized in a friend in our twenties will be very different from what we will be seeking in a partner in our forties or fifties, for instance.

If you look back at what you wanted, say, two, five, or ten years ago, chances are if something remains unfulfilled on that list, you may not want it anymore. Or if you still do, that was the Beta Version. Now you're after 2.0. You changed. And so did your goal.

You are heading into a boundless and limitless future. And a version of you that fits in with that. So, take the time now to give those past goals an MOT check to see if they are still worthy to carry you forward into that future. If not – time to trade them in for the newer, faster, and upgraded version.

SUMMARY

Step Three
Write Your Manifesting Manifesto

- Write it! The pure act of putting pen to paper sets our intention like a magic spell. It puts the Universe on notice that we are serious about what it is we wish to bring into our lives. And acts as a contract with ourselves to set our intention to do just that. This precious manuscript is your divine magical blueprint for your future.
- Start by ordering stuff you truly know you deserve and that you believe can come. I only order what I truly believe is likely. I wouldn't order a white deer, for instance, because although it sounds fabulous in principle, I don't believe it will come and it will need a ten-foot fence!
- Focus your intention. Make this your laser beam of clarity which does not waver. Intention is the master key to unlocking your power to bring that goal into reality.
- Future-proof your wishes! As we change and evolve, so do our goals. Chances are if you're 30 you no longer want what you did when you were 18. Or if you do, the form has changed. Including old goals that no longer serve you diverts that manifesting energy away from drawing what does. Always check whether you still want what you wanted.
- Protect the precious seedlings of those dreams. Just as you need to shelter tender young shoots from the elements, your desires need sunlight, shelter, and love to take root. This means keeping them under glass and protected from those who would rain on them, or simply uproot them before they can bloom. In other words, resist sharing your dreams with others until they have manifested – unless you

are 100 percent certain of their support for what you want to attain.

- Upgrade your goals for relevance. As we evolve, what we desire for ourselves transforms along with us. And even if your goal is still the same as it was five years ago, chances are it looks very different today than it did back then. Update as needed. This is Manifestation 2.0!

ORDER WITH THE JOY AND EXPECTATION OF A CHILD

The simplest step is often the hardest. Ordering with the joy and expectation of a child sends a direct calling signal to manifest your desires. Why? Because it is totally pure. If we can clear away our fears, doubts, and worries and step into a place of innocent trust in the Universe, we are in exactly the right place to become a magnet for our dreams.

But how do we order? Lots of books on manifesting ask you to be VERY SPECIFIC in your order. Having manifested for years, I learned (the hard way) that when we try to take control of a list (especially when it comes to love), we are always going to leave something out. We order a list of the perfect human, but they end up having the breath of a dead wildebeest, or perhaps we forgot to add the word 'honest' to our list. I have conjured many lovers in my time who were everything on my list, but like a fairy-tale catch, there was a forgotten quality that made the relationship impossible.

How do we counteract this? Easy! Ask the cosmos for the right love for you, the ideal match, the yin to your yang, the salmon to your cream cheese. Not only is it easier than writing a long list, it is also foolproof. We still need to use our energy to co-create what we want to draw to us and here is how.

How to Decide What to Order With the Joy of a Child

When we were kids, we believed in magic. We were filled with wonder. We didn't question this. We believed that anything was possible and trusted that magic existed and was real. If we can recapture our awe and wonder, and our belief in the limitless workings of magic, we can remove all blocks to what we want to create.

Play With the Energy

Be spontaneous and cast your seeds of desire into the Universe when you are feeling happy. If you have a moment when you wake up optimistic and enthusiastic, it's the perfect time to go after what you want. Find yourself in nature or on a beach? Run around as if you were a child with no worries and shout your orders into the wind.

Expectation. Anticipation. Manifestation

Manifesting is a collaborative process between you and the Universe. It requires your focused intention and the Universe's responsiveness to bring your desires into reality. Plus your joyful, playful enthusiasm.

One of the essential elements of successful manifesting is the art of expectation. Once you've clearly defined your desire, it's crucial to solidify your intention by wholeheartedly expecting it to come to you. Just like when you were a kid waiting for the tooth fairy to deliver cash under your pillow when you lost a tooth. Think back to moments when you've anticipated something with such eagerness that you could barely contain your excitement. Perhaps it was a cherished event like your birthday or a long-awaited vacation. That same level of joyful anticipation is what amplifies your manifesting power.

The Universe is a vast, responsive energy field and it can sense your belief in its ability to fulfill your desires through that kind of vibrant expectation. Remember, expectation is distinct from impatience. Impatience carries an undercurrent of doubt, while true expectation vibrates with confident certainty. The Universe mirrors back the energy you put out, responding effortlessly to unwavering belief and joyous anticipation.

While you hold that joyful expectation, picture yourself already living your desire. See it in your mind's eye, feel the emotions of having it as if it were already yours. This practice, along with taking actions that align with your goals, will supercharge it.

A fabulous illustration of this is the joyful way Jim Carrey created his superstardom. Before Jim Carrey was lighting up the world with his unique humor as one of the most famous actors of the 1990s, he had a secret manifesting weapon – ordering with the joy and expectation of a child. He chose Mulholland Drive, one of the most famous roads in LA. It has unrivaled views of the city below and is where creatives and millionaires live. This was his personal stage for visualizing his wildest dreams. Staring at the city lights, he would stand there, arms flung wide open to the Universe, and declare, 'I'm a sought-after actor; every director wants to work with me!' He didn't just say it, he believed it with every fiber of his being. He only left when he believed it, that it was true; only then would he drive home excited and triumphant.

His next step was writing himself a check for $10 million. A cheque for 'acting services rendered.' Not just a piece of paper, it was a manifesto, a constant reminder of his unwavering ambition and his TRUST in the future. That childlike belief delivered when he was paid the exact sum of $10 million for the movie *The Mask*.

Run, play, holler it out loud. Find situations that make you feel blissful and use that innocent ecstasy to blast out your orders.

ACTION STEP

Happiness Is Your Truth

Self-love is an essential key to manifesting. If we don't love ourselves, an essential spice in the manifesting recipe is missing. It's a cinnamon bun without the cinnamon. Self-love is an ongoing process: we don't just wake up one day and that's it. When we do love ourselves, everything becomes easier, especially happiness. We are constantly bombarded with information that can impact our happiness and our experience in the moment. The good news is that we can become superstars of tweaking external experiences to keep our happiness levels high.

1. What do you really feel about yourself? How can you heal yourself to welcome in more self-love? What is blocking you from feeling worthy? How do you express your love for yourself? Do you believe with all of your being that you deserve happiness?
2. Examine what happiness really is. For instance, some people say they want to win the lottery and I always ask why. It's never about the money but about what people think the money will bring. But listening to what people who have won the lottery have to say undermines the idea that money automatically brings happiness. It doesn't. Many lottery winners claim that winning actually ruined their lives and they genuinely wish it had never happened. Some say that having money stirred up a

lot of issues around trust as it made it hard for them to know who actually loved them and who only wanted to be around their money. Others say that no matter how much they spent, it did not bring them happiness. This is not only fascinating but a clue to a deeper truth: it is not money in and of itself that can buy peace of mind.

3. Using your psychic intuition, go within and look at other ways that happiness and fulfillment can come. Let go of cultural ideas that physical appearance, money, and fame are what bring joy. Cast that from your mind. Go back to your core values because those are your happiness seeds. And from these, your deeper desires and what gives you joy and pleasure emerge. Be still for a moment and visualize yourself happy, at peace, and inspired. You'll be amazed at how rarely having 'stuff' features in this. No matter what our current situation is, we can find a deeper peace by connecting to our refuge of joy. What is your vibration telling the Universe? And what would you like the Universe to hear?

4. One scientific study mapped people's happiness levels and concluded that we are only happy when we are present in the moment. Rather than dream your life away, revel in the present, feel totally alive in it. Look to the moment for your joy. The present is a gift and within it find a way to raise your vibration to follow and create your dreams.

5. What you read, listen to, and watch affects your vibration. If something is making you feel bad, avoid it. Read books that inspire you and stimulate you. Watch something uplifting. Or that simply makes you laugh. Seek out what inspires you. Whatever your current situation, focus on taking practical steps to make your dreams come true. Being utterly present in the moment rather

than choosing escapism allows us to find the gift, the blessing, the wonder in our lives. Believe me, it is there.

6. Happiness is not only a choice we make but also a spiritual experience. Happiness is the 'ten thousand joys' we are told to expect in Buddhism. There's a lot of guilt we may have been taught around being happy. Old beliefs can die hard. Many people still hang on to the outdated belief that lack and suffering place one on a 'higher' spiritual path. We are here to experience all that life offers us and this includes the sweet gifts as well as the salty and sour. Feeling guilty about claiming what makes us happy automatically stops the flow of it.

7. What did you love to do as a child? What activity can you lose yourself in? One that allows you to enter that effortless state of 'flow'? One you lose all track of time with when engaging in it? Did you give it up because you were made to feel it was 'childish'? Or do you constantly tell yourself you'll 'make time' for fun once you've attended to other things? Is it time to take fun seriously and make time for it?

PRO TIP

When we are doing what we love, our energy is at its most open and our minds at their most receptive. We are at one with ourselves and the infinite flow of the Universe. It doesn't matter whether we're building that Lego model, painting, or walking on the beach – we are in our joy and happy. There's no better mindset for the Universe to work its wonders. Doing what makes us happy puts us in our most powerful attraction state.

 **SUMMARY**

Step Four
Order with the Joy and Expectation of a Child

- The simplest act holds the most power. Ordering your desires with childlike joy sends a clear message to the Universe. Why? Because it's a pure, unfiltered belief. When we let go of doubt and fear, embracing a playful trust in the Universe, we become a potent magnet for our visions. Make it fun and lighthearted, and believe like a child.

- Self-love is your power tool of joy and abundance. When we truly love ourselves – which is very different from self-entitlement and narcissism – we stop comparing ourselves to others, stop being envious, and stop crazy and energy-draining attempts to be accepted for anyone other than we truly are. In other words – Just the Way You Are becomes your superpower and the way to effortless attraction.

- Choose happiness because you and your child within deserve it. There are a lot of miserable millionaires out there. Equally, there are many people who have less, materially, who would describe themselves as extremely happy. Yes, we can encounter setbacks and challenges along the way which can temporarily impact our ability to feel joy. But it's exactly that – temporary. See yourself as vibrant and happy and this becomes your default setting.

- Cultivate a 'gift' mentality, and to be cheesy ha-ha, that's why this moment is called 'the present'.

- Happiness is when you are expressing your truth. Unfiltered and uncaring what others may think. See happiness as not just your birthright but a spiritual practice in its own right. When you are happy, you are at your most open and receptive to receiving what the Universe wants to send your way.

STEP FIVE

CONNECT WITH YOUR FUTURE SELF

Take a minute to think about yourself in the past. Look back to a sticky situation in your teenage years and think about what advice you would give to your younger self. I often visualize and talk to my younger self. Whenever I am really happy or have achieved a goal, I send love and wisdom to that lost feral child. I truly believe that I have received that wisdom in some way and it's transformed me and is continuing to do so.

It might be difficult to get your head around, but the current scientific thinking is that we might live in a multiverse where every decision we make is happening in a different dimension and there are hundreds and thousands of worlds with different versions of us in them. Incredibly, there is nothing in the laws of physics to state that time should move in the forward direction that we know, and indeed it is probably 'Everything, Everywhere, All At Once'. Don't worry too much about understanding the science behind the theory, just use it to your advantage to boost your belief.

Healing and talking to our past self could have an impact on our future. As nuts as that sounds, I have experienced intense healing through this lifelong practice. However, there is another way to use this knowledge. And through sharing this technique in workshops over the years, I have seen it produce extraordinary results.

Let's take that one step further. Imagine if you could connect with your future self. A future self that has succeeded and wants to support you. To recap, science tells us that in the quantum field, all of time is relative. In other words, it is all happening right now. And time is something we have come up with to stop everything from happening all at once. Which means, in theory, that we can psychically project ourselves anywhere we want to go. At any time. In no time at all. So, if we take this one step further, you already have what you are setting out to manifest. Trippy, right?

One of my fascinations with this theory is that this might, in the future, explain and hopefully prove how manifesting works, by having the ability to link into this timelessness. But how can we take advantage of this theory right now? Within our somewhat limited perception of what time is?

No one is suggesting we can hail an Uber to take us into the future anytime soon. Yet can we use this theory to transform our life and bring us into our power today? Can we play with the concept of timelessness to enhance our life right now? The answer is most definitely yes! As Carlo Rovelli says in *The Order of Time*, our idea of time is illusory, something we've constructed, rather than how it actually behaves in the physical universe.

One of my most potent techniques for manifesting is writing a letter from your future self in which you describe the life you are living in, say, a year's time.

I shared this technique at a workshop I conducted at the Mind Body Spirit Festival in London in 2011. A year later, I received so many emails telling me how amazed people were when they received their letters – many of the predictions in them had come true. In fact, 11 years later, I bumped into someone who told me that in that workshop, they made a specific request to find a partner. Someone who was a musician and also a family man. Not only did she find a love who matched that description, they married and had been together for 10 years and were still madly in love.

Take a moment to imagine what goals you have manifested a year from now. How and where will you be living? With whom? What job will you be doing? How will your life look? And most importantly, who have you become now you are living that life? How do you look? What do you feel? Don't focus just on the changes you wish to bring about. Focus on how these have changed you. From the inside out. And revel in the emotional state that is this future you's reality.

Now, think back to five years ago and imagine that you had written a similar letter to yourself to be mailed to you five years in the future. How different does your life look today than it did back then? What goals did you attain? What turned out better than you could possibly have imagined? What have you yet to accomplish? Or have you achieved everything you set out to do back then and have embarked on new goals?

There's a point to this. When we set out and write these letters from our future selves, we are, in fact, setting a deadline to achieve our goals. It's strange because normally, when we set out our goals, we either omit to put in a deadline or just the idea of it is so scary we shy away from it. Yes, believe it or not, very often the thing we want the most is also the thing that scares us the most. Why? Because it takes us out of our comfort zone and away from what's familiar. Even if what's familiar is no good for us or blatantly toxic.

Throw Yourself a Manifestation Lifeline

Sometimes, though not always, setting a hard deadline is a vital part of the process. It puts the Universe and our higher selves on alert that there is a cut-off point to be met here. No pressure! But if the term 'deadline' pushes buttons for you, what if we call it 'lifeline' instead? 'Lifeline' conjures up an image of something that keeps us buoyant and afloat. A direct link between where you are right now with the future you are envisioning for yourself. One that not only keeps you on course but keeps tugging you toward your desired outcome over your given time period. Doesn't that sound like it's a supportive part of the process as opposed to a ticking clock or schedule you have to adhere to – or else fail miserably?

So, where do you want to be one year from now? Get out your journal and write this down in note form to begin with. We will get to the lifeline letter later. Once you're done, go back over what you've written down and think about it for a moment. What are you doing RIGHT NOW about achieving these goals? Or what can you do that you might have been putting off? Or has this exercise kick-started your creative thought process and you can already see actions you can begin to take which had not occurred to you until you started writing?

Most importantly, take a moment to ask yourself why you are trying to achieve them. What need do they fill for you? Is there a goal behind your goal or is there another goal that would meet your need far more effectively?

For example, let's just say that your goal is to be on the cover of a magazine. Why do you have this goal? Is it that then you will know you have 'made it'? Is it to make your mum proud of you or show everyone out there who has ever been mean to you or rejected you just how wrong they were? Write down all of this and do this for every goal you want to see manifest over your lifeline period. This can be for a year or even five years in the future. How long is up to you. But you must have an 'Achieve By' date in mind. And a realistic one. So – please don't set dates for more than five years in the future as that is, in fact, opting out and telling the Universe that what you want is impossible.

Now, let's go back to why you want to achieve your goals and return to the example I gave you before – you want to be on the cover of a magazine. Why? Is it a milestone that represents the fact that you have 'made it' in your chosen field – be it *Fast Company*, *Wired*, *Hello!*, *Rolling Stone*, *The Hollywood Reporter*, *Vogue*, or *Forbes*? Or is it a revenge goal where all the meanies get to see how fabulously successful you now are and how wrong and insignificant they are? Be honest. Because honesty is a key part of knowing thyself. And do this without judgment.

Now, imagine all the other ways that would also give you an equal feeling of having reached the top. List these. Tap into the feeling that they bring you. Is it equal to your original goal? Or does it make you feel even more alive and excited at the prospect of reaching it? If so, you just found the real goal you should be manifesting.

Keep asking why you want what you want. Even with new goals on your list. Is it because you want someone's love or approval? If so, you now have some serious thinking to do since if they don't love and/or approve of you now, why are you so determined you need to impress them? Either you have their love now or you don't. Becoming a billionaire or getting your photo on the cover of *Vanity Fair* will not change that. Don't waste your energy trying to change other people's opinions about you. The only opinion that matters is yours.

If you want that goal for yourself, however, keep it on your list. If not, reject it. This is all part of the Lifeline process. It's not just about setting deadlines. A Lifeline is just that – it supports you. It is your unbreakable link between you and all you can manifest. Do this with every goal on your list. Once you have put each and every one of them through this process, it's now time to weave your Lifeline.

ACTION STEP

Get a Lifeline

Write that letter to yourself, putting the future date you have decided on at the top. State not only your goals but the things you started doing to achieve them. For example, 'I started back in August (add year) by doing research on the companies I should approach. And then came up with a strategy to contact them which I had set in motion by (add date).' Go into details about the fabulous experiences on the way, the flashes of brilliance that got you there.

When you have done that, sign and seal your letter, address it to yourself, and give it to a friend or relative you trust to mail it to you on your future date (write this on the envelope). If you are using a website such as FutureMe to email you your letter, when you compose it you can set the date on which they will send it to you. You have now created not a deadline but a Lifeline between your present and your future destination. It's not just a line but a straight path you can now follow – directly to your desires.

You may be surprised when you receive your letter not only by how things turned out but how much better they turned out than you could possibly have imagined. But your commitment and setting that Lifeline were the catalysts which set it all in motion. Be prepared to take whatever actions you need for success and, above all, be determined to fearlessly step into that new future you have created right now. Above all, know that your past – and that includes who you were in that past – does not determine what that future looks like.

If You Want to Change Your Energy in the Moment, Here Is an Instant Vibration Hack

Find somewhere quiet and comfortable. Switch off your phone – this is sacred Do Not Disturb time. Sit down and close your eyes.

Imagine your life as a long road – with the past stretching out one way and the future heading off in another. Where you are standing right now on that road is the present. In the present you can pivot. You can look up or down the road.

Turn and face the direction of your past. Set your mind to draw your attention to all of those times when you felt great – happy, excited, joyful. Those moments of bliss when life flowed your way. And when you thought anything was possible for you. Get a sense of where those times are along your life's road. They might shine out like twinkling stars or just stand out in some other way like illuminated signs along a highway beckoning you to pull in and visit like a roadside attraction. Imagine yourself revisiting them. Re-experiencing those fabulous feelings from the highlighted events in your past. And noticing how they change your mood as you go.

Hold those emotions. When you feel you are totally reliving them, gather them up and come back to the present on your Lifeline's highway. Look at the road ahead of you and turn your psychic attention to the future. Set your intention for a specific point in the future. Maybe the date of an upcoming event where you want to be at your very best. Or perhaps just a period away from the present which covers your Lifeline time span when you expect to make the changes which lead to your goal.

Start to move forward toward that point. As you do, trust that deep, at a cellular level, you are processing all the information you'll need to take you from the present to the future you want to create. When you reach the point you were heading toward, stop and rest a while. Look back to see how far you've come. Also notice anything interesting that you might want to take conscious note of to bring back to the present.

Return to that point now. Ground yourself firmly by getting up and moving around, while holding on to all of those good feelings that you've gathered along your way.

You can repeat this experiment any time by picking a point in your future and gathering up your happiness and positive memories to take with you. Look around you when you get there. Pay attention to the detail. Are there others who are waiting for you when you arrive at that point? Do you already know them? Or have you yet to encounter them at a future time? Write down who or what you see. Ask your future self for more details on how to get there from right where you are now. Know that you have in fact already arrived simply by starting this process.

When you begin this particular exercise, you may enjoy taking your time to do it. Especially when it comes to reliving happy moments and experiencing the exciting future that you want to create for yourself. But as you progress, you set your speed. You can choose to fast forward or simply allow it to unwind in its own time. This is something that you can train yourself to do in a couple of minutes and incorporate easily into a busy schedule – anywhere and at any time, without creating a huge ritual around it. Or you can luxuriate in your process. Whatever works for you.

All of us drift off into the past and then imagine our future. Often on a daily basis. This process taps right into what we are already adept at doing. But this way we use it to our quantum advantage.

Connect with your future self: what are you doing in X years' time? Be specific: how does your future look and feel? Where are you living, who are you spending time with, what brings you joy, and why? How have these changes in your life changed you: how does future you feel in future you's reality? How did you get there? Write a letter from your future detailing all that you have achieved and how you did it. You can write it for one, five, ten, any number of years. Seal the envelope and post it to yourself after the allotted time has passed. Your future self is always there to advise you.

Time Travel for Dummies

We've gone back in time and allowed our present selves to give who we were in the past the unconditional love and support we were lacking back then. We've then leapt forward and imagined who we will become and where we will be at very specific dates in the future. We've date-stamped our intentions like setting a date on the controls of that time machine.

The future is, in fact, happening right now. And in this moment is when we are creating it. But we're not doing this alone. You've met your Future Self. Now, get ready to meet your co-creators.

 SUMMARY

Step Five
Connect With Your Future Self

- Time travel! If all versions of you exist simultaneously, then see the future version of you as a resource you can connect with at any time. Not only can you use your vision of who you will become as your touchstone for goal success, Future You is available at all times to answer questions on how you made it.
- Time is a river that flows both ways. You can also go back in time and revisit your past self. Imagine giving them the love or support you were denied back then. In doing so, you not only empower present you, you actively change the course of all your futures.
- Writing letters to your Future Self is an excellent way to set goal deadlines. In your letters, you can describe in detail

where you are on your journey at the time of writing. And then take that leap forward, say, six months into the future. Choose a specific goal or goals that you want to have manifested by that date. Don't overload your resources, however. Five should be your maximum for this exercise. You don't need to go into details of just how you achieved them. Leave the Universe room to work its magic! But by the time that letter finds you in the future, you'll be astounded at how much you have accomplished.

- Use pleasurable feelings and times you have experienced success in the past as an emotional GPS to guide you toward more of those experiences on your future path.
- Bear in mind the future is not set in stone. And it is certainly not defined by our past. We can change our future at any point. Simply by changing our minds. Manifestation is the ultimate mind-changing tool. Because when we decide to manifest something better for ourselves, we automatically shift our future path.
- I stumbled across this site where you can write a letter to your future self at futureme.org. The site not only allows you to set a date in the future when you will receive your letter (three months, six months, or a year), it stores previous letters you have written to your future self so you can reread them and see just how far you've come.

STEP SIX

EMBRACE CO-CREATION POWER

I have been fascinated by the power of group contagion and how our interactions with others profoundly influence our lives. We all have our unique belief systems, we are all part of the whole, but are a unique shard of it, like a single cell in a giant organism.

Our job is to explore our uniqueness to express our individuality while knowing we are inextricably connected to the whole. Each of us brings something different to this glorious human party. The more we honor our true selves, the easier it is to manifest. Plus, our job is to explore our uniqueness, which helps evolve the whole. When we grow and explore, so can others. Simple, right? So how do we do it and how can we stop ourselves being hijacked by negative beliefs?

I was in two minds about writing about social contagion as at the time of writing the term has been hijacked by various political parties to condemn or minimize support for those that are marginalized or protesting. This shows how dangerous ideas can be if a group uses them for its own shady purposes.

Back in 2010 when I was researching for a talk I was doing, I came across a book which blew my mind, *Connected: The Amazing Power of Social Networks and How They Shape Our Lives* by Nicholas Christakis and James Fowler, which reinforced everything I believed about our incredible impact on each other. Here are a few of the key takeaways.

It's not just your immediate friends and family who shape your life. The effects of our social network spread up to three degrees of separation (your friends' friends' friends). These connections influence everything from our happiness to our career prospects. Smoking habits and even voting patterns can spread through social networks like a virus. At first this sounds wild, unbelievable, yet many different studies have found this to be true.

The health, happiness, and success of the people we spend time with indirectly yet profoundly influence our lives. This can greatly benefit or hinder our manifesting. Which is why it's essential to choose our connections wisely. It is so easy to forget this. Think back to a time when you knew in your heart that inviting someone to a party was a bad idea. But you bowed to peer pressure (or your guilt for excluding them), only for it to end up a disaster. One person has the ability to poison the vibes of a group.

Our actions and decisions have ripple effects, positively or negatively influencing people we have never met. Just like a virus can spread through a population, behaviors, emotions, and ideas can spread through a social network. One person's happiness can infect their friend, who in turn influences their other connections, creating a domino effect.

Picture this. You are at a fantastic lunch with your best pals. The next day you catch a cold and then several of your friends at the gathering also fall ill. They then pass it on to their other friends and family, and onwards it goes. We can't see the cold virus, we have no clue which one of our friends passed it on. Similarly, our social influence extends far beyond those we know directly. A simple act of kindness or a shared political opinion can whiz through your network and reach people you'll likely never meet.

We are happily oblivious that our friends, their friends, and even further connections have an impact on us. Just like we might not always know how we caught a cold, the indirect social forces shaping our decisions are invisible yet powerful.

A study by the University of California analyzed 100 million people and 1 billion status updates on Facebook and discovered that our updates cause emotional changes in our network. But that brilliant news, positive posts creating positive mood changes spread the quickest. When we are kind, upbeat, and optimistic, we are influencing hundreds of people we don't know.

If you couple this with the power of mirror neurons (when we watch something on TV or another human, our brain lights up in the exact same way as a person eating a salad, having sex, picking up a ball, as if we were physically doing the same thing) and brain entrainment (where we can chant, sing, or concentrate – a group will naturally synchronize their brain waves as if they were one), we can see how we are deeply, inextricably linked.

One of the reasons this is important is that we can then be vigilant to keep our unique voice and beliefs clear. It also allows us to plug into the whole and draw our dreams to us. If we KNOW we are this connected, then by paying careful attention to what we want to 'catch' from others (detoxing our thoughts and beliefs regularly), taking care of what is in our minds, in the same way we take care of our body while knowing that it works both ways. We have a secret superpower here: we can tap into this universal network to call in coincidences and people that help us. We know it is possible. It gives us permission and shows us the importance of expressing our uniqueness.

The power of groups can be used for good or bad. We've seen that group dynamics and attitudes can be contagious and have a profound effect on our lives. The good news is, we can take advantage of this to superboost our manifesting. If you feel that you don't have a group of friends to do this step, you can reach out to find new people ready to share a joint manifesting adventure. By now you have the skills to manifest them! Ask the Universe to send you three or four people who have a similar or inspiring energy and know they are coming (don't forget to do the work and ask around and look for them).

So why are groups of people so powerful? Let's look at a scientific understanding and a spiritual one.

How Group Projections Become Real

If a group projects an idea onto something or someone, they bring that idea into reality. It takes on physical form. If someone moves into a small village, the present residents already have opinions of all the people who live there. We may be told 'He's wonderful' or 'She's horrible'. We may not have met them yet, but to a certain extent our preconceptions about them have already been set. So, when we meet the person, we look for signs that validate what we have been told. After all, if so many people agree, it must be true. We start a new job and several people point out that someone is unpopular, not a team player, uncool, or not 'normal'. To be included as part of the group, we are then expected to go along with their version of reality.

Not only does group projection like this seek to influence us rather than allow us to make up our own mind, but all that negative energy dehumanizes the person it is directed at. Making us complicit. And worse, the person themselves may end up believing it. If others repeatedly make you feel strange or excluded, in the end that is how you see yourself. Equally, if the message you receive is that you are kind, you will grow into more kindness. If you feel accepted and validated, you become more confident and outgoing.

Group energy is potent influence. And it applies to nearly all group situations. We create an idea and collaboration of thought and then beam it onto the people we encounter. We can assume it has to be true if the entire group agrees. And so group reality becomes ours. After all, isn't it easier to go along with that rather than being the one thought 'weird' or excluded? It's easy to underestimate the power of this kind of group projection. But it can have a life-long impact on us. Often, people who felt bullied or picked on in a school environment carry that underlying wound into adult life.

In a study led by a team at the Max Planck Institute for Evolutionary Anthropology in Leipzig, Germany, and published in *Psychological Science*, it was discovered that the desire to conform is probably something we are born with. An experiment conducted with two-year-olds as well as with chimps and orangutans revealed that humans have a natural desire to conform even if it takes away their individual pleasure. In the experiments, chimps, orangutans, and children were asked to drop a ball into a box divided into three sections, one of which always resulted in a reward (chocolate for the children, a peanut for the apes). After the kids and apes realized that they got a reward if they put the ball in the right box, they then watched a group of their peers do the same thing – but in this case their peers did not get a reward.

When the original group was given their next turn, the group who did not get a reward was watching them. This time, 50 percent of the children appeared to deliberately put the ball in the wrong box. However, the apes didn't care and carried on putting the ball in the box that earned them peanuts. It wasn't that the children had forgotten which box gave them the yummy chocolate, because when the children were not being watched by the group that got no chocolate, they tended to switch back to putting the ball in the correct reward box. In other words, even at this young age, the desire to appear to conform overrode the desire for a chocolate. At least for half of the group.

Another profound experiment in this area demonstrates the uncanny power of group influence. The Asch Experiment was first used in the 1950s but has been repeated many times with the same result. In this case, there is a person in a group who does not know that the others are part of the experiment. Everyone is asked a simple question (which is the longest of three lines). The answer is very obvious as one line is clearly longer than the other two. But when the whole group gives the wrong answer, the unwitting loner ends up agreeing with the rest of the group against blatant logic and the evidence of their own eyes. Shockingly, this is how ingrained our desire to conform can be.

Are we therefore trapped by our desire to fit in? Is this so deeply rooted that we're not even aware of how often we do it? Are we so hard-wired by evolution to survive by strengthening community ties that we end up making decisions in our adult life which impact our free will and rob us of our freedom and individuality? Because the power of group beliefs and ideas can dramatically impact our ability to manifest. You can check on this right now. How would the people around you react if you created your dream life and were living it? Whether as a group or on an individual basis? The thing is, you already know. Or your higher self does. Run through the names of the people you know. Or a group of them. The reaction you feel within when you think of them tells you instantly who would celebrate for you. And who would cluster together behind your back to share their resentment and jealousy.

If we encounter a group situation where someone is the target of mass energy projection, do honor their energy and yours by taking a step back and seeing the person as if you had not heard the group dream of them. Maintain your right to make up your own mind. Yes, you may very well end up agreeing with them. But none of us can be defined in black-and-white terms. Your experience of them may run contrary to the group's. If that is the case, stand by it. You may be the catalyst for a whole new group mindset.

Yes, people can more easily live up to our best expectations of them than our low ones. It always pays to look for the love and goodness within others, rather than any negative traits. But if you sense that the truth is that someone does not have your back, choose instead those who do. We are self-creating beings and it is not just our own views but those of others that mold our present, our future, and our idea of who we are.

The Science

Empathy is crucial to society and of course is one of the great spiritual qualities. Shaman have always told us that we are all connected. Quantum physics might tell us that science agrees this is so. But empathy lets us feel it for ourselves. And there is scientific proof that we really are all connected.

We all have motor neurones at the front of our brain that fire up when we perform an action, such as doing a yoga pose or pouring a coffee. The big discovery came when scientists realized that some of those neurones would also fire up in our brains when someone did something in front of us. In other words, if you reach for an apple in front of me, some of the motor neurones that would fire up if I reached for an apple (or anything else) would spark up in my brain. This process of what happens in the brain between people is called mirror neurones. A neuroscientist called V.S. Ramachandran thinks that these have played a huge role in evolution, and especially the evolution of culture, as this means that if I develop a new skill and do it in front of you, just watching me puts your brain in rehearsal for actually doing it yourself.

More importantly, Ramachandran talks about some of the same neurones firing up in our brains when we watch someone else being touched that would fire up if we were being touched. He says that if we then block the receptors that tell the brain it's not actually us being touched, we have no way of knowing who is being touched. We only feel what others are feeling, essentially linking us all together.

What that means is that even though we are individuals, our connection to the whole is just as important to the nature of our very existence. In fact, our brain is hard-wired to link into the whole to a point where we actually need other circuits to remind us that we are separate. As Ramachandran says, the absolute scientific reality is that the only thing separating all of us is our skin.

The Importance and Power of Focus

Did you know that an atom does not exist in one place until it is measured? During experiments, if a human observer does not measure the atom, it exists in many places at once. Focusing on the atom makes it change how it behaves and become 'real'. This is called the observer effect and it is a clear illustration of the power of focus and consciousness to create reality. What is astounding is that this isn't woo-woo thinking, this is a scientific fact.

We are all not only creating our own reality but co-creating the reality of the entire world. What we choose to believe is drawn toward us. What we think and how we feel spreads out and hooks up with other people's beliefs and feelings. You could say we are all participating in one big, shared dream. If you know how to tap into your place within this, you can draw to you a whole host of new experiences and start to draw toward you your own dream of what reality looks like.

As we can see, none of us is immune to the dreams or influence of others as we're all magical beings together. Our energy functions as an interconnected whole. And each part ripples out onto the next. Surrounding yourself with people that recognize your power and your beauty helps you grow into your power and your beauty. As you enable them to do the same.

We don't only create on our own. The collective, our culture, and especially the people we are close to have a huge impact on how we create our future lives. We've talked about the frenemy within us. And how to change that dialogue and our relationship to it. So, it's vital to take an honest inventory of how the people around you impact your life. And to weed out the energy vampires or those determined to rain on your parade or negate your dreams.

Of course, some of these weeds are a little more persistent in our lives, for example that suffocating colleague who doesn't respect your boundaries or the interfering neighbor from hell. We all have these relation obligations in our lives that we can't escape from. However, once you have identified who these people are, you will be in a stronger position to defend your energy and protect your power – and that's the thing, when you reclaim your power from these types of people, it is extremely freeing.

We've talked about how releasing those old patterns plays a major role in unleashing our manifesting power. Well, group energy can help with this as well. Especially if you know other manifesting magicians!

Hanging onto the past stops us from appreciating the present and creating the future we desire. We all carry baggage from our past, but we should take care not to travel into the future weighed down with stuff we no longer need. I'm not talking about throwing out that beloved childhood teddy bear or those photographs. But that outfit you rocked back as a teenager. Those love letters your ex wrote you seven years ago and you've not seen or heard from them in three? We invest our energy in these things but get no return. Time to reclaim it and start living in the now by decluttering the past.

You're Invited to a Letting Go Party

Yes, of course you can clear out the clutter and what you no longer need on your own. But if you know like-minded souls committed to manifesting their own miracles, then why not get together and have a releasing party?

Group energy is a powerful thing. The more people who participate, the more it puts the Universe on notice that you are part of a powerful dynamic open to change. And it also helps supercharge the process for all of you.

Each of you can bring significant items which represent your old selves, a period in your lives you are glad to be leaving behind, or which are symbolic of something you no longer need, want to attract, or have outgrown. Your teenage diaries where you unloaded all that hormonal angst and unhappiness. Those skinny jeans from your fashion-victim era. The tea towel your ex gave you (true story!). Choose something that has an emotional charge to it and is linked in your mind with what needs to be released and not repeated.

Show and tell. Of course, I'm not saying you have to read long extracts from those diaries and reveal all those wounds and vulnerabilities if you are not comfortable doing so. You can instead talk in general terms about what was happening in your life back then. And how you are now ready to gain closure by letting this item go.

Some items you may choose to donate or sell afterward (ensure you do this and as soon as possible – don't hang on to them. No excuses!). Others, like those old love letters or that private diary, you can choose to burn in a fire-proof brazier. By all means, smash that horrific vase your ex-mother-in-law gifted you. Especially if it represents everything that was wrong with your marriage. I know of someone who burned the granny pants her former mother-in-law gave her one Christmas. The pants were a size 20. She's a size 8 (another true story).

Each of you can share your associations with what you are releasing with other members of the group. And why it is now so important for you to consign the items to the past now.

Cutting Cords

Attachments to other people can take shape energetically through cords that attach us through the quantum soup to others. If you feel that you can't 'let go' of someone, take time when you won't be disturbed, close your eyes, and focus your intention by taking in and exhaling three deep breaths.

Visualize that other person at a safe distance (as safe as you want it – you can have them a million miles away and this will still work) and see if you can notice any thick or thin cords that run between you both. In your mind, say, 'I release you with love for the highest good of all,' and imagine something such as a knife or scissors cutting through those cords.

No matter how this person has hurt you or what they have done, it's best to release them with love for them and, most importantly, for you. Bless them, send them on their way, which leaves you free to go yours.

Fire Rituals

If you have access to somewhere you can safely light a fire, such as an open grate or fire pit in the garden, you can use this to literally burn away the old. You can burn a letter to the Universe about what you want to release. If you are trying to release a person or a past event, write out all of the pain, anger, grief, or whatever it is you are feeling. Write until you get to a place of peace and end it expressing your gratitude that this has now been lifted from your life.

Write out any beliefs that limit your ability to attract love. You can burn all of these on the fire. You can also burn anything that represents what you are trying to release, such as photographs or small mementos. You can throw a handful of sage into the fire as it is fantastic for cleansing. When the fire is out and cold, scatter or bury the ashes. If you don't have anywhere that you can safely light a fire, you can do the whole thing through visualization just as effectively.

Positive Group Contagion

Group Power = Sharing the dream

Now let's talk about the astonishing power of groups. So how can we use this for good? We know that the power of sharing your dream with others is especially potent. In my 'Cosmic Ordering' DVD that I created in 2005, I talked about a technique I used in my manifesting workshops. I would interview participants, or participants would interview each other in a chat-show style. Those being interviewed were asked about a dream they held but talked about it as though it had already come true.

You use the same neural pathways in your brain to process stuff about the past, present, and future. And also what is real and what is imaginary. In other words, as far as your brain is concerned, it cannot differentiate between something that you imagine and something that has really happened. Imagining a future that you're working toward as if it has already happened gives you an enormous magical boost. This is a technique favored in sports psychology, where athletes are encouraged to visualize themselves performing at their peak as a way of maximizing their ability to win when the time comes for them to actually get out on the field or track.

So, when you speak about a goal as if it has already manifested, you are not only giving yourself a boost, but because your brain perceives this as your reality, you now have access to neural pathways which help you find creative solutions to the details that you might not have cracked yet.

Everyone is different. And we'd all like to think that we are totally independent of the views of others. But again, the idea that labels stick and have an effect is something that social psychologists recognize. You are now going to give yourself a high-gloss, high-status label by imagining yourself as the main guest on a chat show. Where you are treated as someone successful and brilliant with an inspiring story to tell. Seeing yourself in this situation will actually help you unlock all those qualities within you.

1. Find at least one friend you can do it with, someone from your support network. This is actually a really fun thing to do as a group too. The ultimate fame night in!
2. Make the setting as real as possible. Arrange your furniture so that you have a nice backdrop behind you. Your couch or a couple of comfy chairs are ideal. Set the mood with your lighting. If this is a group exercise, arrange chairs for your 'audience'.

3. Make sure you dress for the occasion. How would you look if you were going to be interviewed on the biggest Netflix show? Give yourself the full star treatment beforehand. Dressing in that outfit that shouts 'success story' is all part and parcel of treating yourself as something precious and important. And that you have actually arrived. Encourage anyone participating in this with you to do the same. This is an event. You are making history. And how you look and feel makes a big difference to the experience.

4. Take it in turns to be in the interviewee's chair. If you are being interviewed, decide how you're going to sum up your dream in one line, whether it's opening your own restaurant or becoming a professional portrait painter or cake decorator. If you are the interviewer, be enthusiastic – give lots of praise and positive feedback and ask questions that encourage the flow of talk. Keep the questions coming. Did they always know they were destined for success? How did they begin? What were the highs and lows? What advice do they have for others who are embarking on their own journey? If you see your subject dry up, move on and then take them back later. If you're in the 'audience', you can do your bit by giving loads of support and applause at all the right moments.

5. If you can, ask someone to video the whole thing. Or if it is just the two of you, set up your phones to record it. Also have your journals handy. This is especially easy for audience members who can quickly jot down gems that spring to mind during interviews. Share these with others afterward.

Whether this is a one-to-one experience or a group exercise, it unleashes all the positive potential waiting to be expressed. And shows you what happens when we choose labels that support each other's dreams. The power of just one other person or many, hearing, cheering, and supporting our future selves, gives us that added level of validation and makes our experience real. As we step into the role of manifestor and creator of our dreams.

ACTION STEP

Soulpreneurs

Are you still working at drawing in your co-creators and soul support group? That's okay. You can still harness the expansive energy of this exercise by yourself. See yourself as a soulpreneur or innovator. And instead of imagining yourself being interviewed on a chat show, act out your very own TED Talk.

You're presenting to a captive audience – people who want to know the secret to your success. The stages you went through. And to be inspired by your story. Just as you would if you were featured on the world's biggest podcast/Netflix show in a group setting, ensure you look your best. Sure, nobody else may see this. But as we've discussed, feeling it is part of being it.

Imagine yourself stepping onto the stage in a crowded auditorium. The applause greets you. Behind you is a giant screen, on to which are projected images of you at key stages of your manifesting journey. You lead your audience through the incredible highs. Share your challenges. And the moments when inspiration struck and you had your breakthrough.

Telling your story TED style also allows you to fine-tune your manifestation process. You'll find that as you speak, more ideas come to you. Share these as if this was a live event. As you speak, notice how your vision and enthusiasm fire up your audience. You can feel the impact you've had by the wave of applause that washes over you as you finish.

You can video this on your phone. Don't be afraid of stopping and starting again if you're not happy with how it's going. And remember – nobody will ever see this unless you want them to. You can film as many takes as you like until you're completely happy with it. What's more – you can now replay it as often as you need until you have the result you're after. You may be astounded by how your journey to getting there mirrors how you tell your 'audience' you did it.

Choose Your Co-Creators

The Universe uses people as its delivery system. Which is why friends, connections, networks, and communities are so important in the manifestation process. People are our greatest asset. Just as they can support us or are the conduits through which our goals are channeled, we perform the same function for others. We are all engaged in creating a collective dream. Individually tailored to our bespoke visions.

We've talked about the need to treat our goals as fragile plants. And not expose them to the negative elements of criticism, doubt, and shade that others can throw our way. While most people we know or encounter will shower us with support and encouragement, not everyone is able to step up into the co-creator paradigm. Which is why we need to choose our connections wisely. And ensure that those we keep or allow in, align with and support our energy. Not drain it.

ACTION STEP

Declutter Your Circle

If we want to attract something new and manifest what truly aligns with our soul into our lives, then we need to make space for it.

It's not just the negative beliefs, the clutter in those drawers, or the stuff in our closets we no longer use that we need to toss, although this is an important part of preparing to manifest something new. But what is equally, if not even more, important is identifying the people around us who don't just throw shade but feed off us energetically. Leaving us drained, disillusioned, and disempowered.

Unleash Your Inner Vampire Hunter

You're a fearless energy vampire hunter intent on banishing the soul-suckers from your life. Here's how to spot one.

Energy Vampires
All of us have experienced at least one of these shady creatures at one time or another. That friend or lover who only ever talks

about themselves, their problems and ongoing dramas. These souls are not fang-tastic – but draining. They expect us always to be there for them, yet when the situation is reversed and we need them, they are either unavailable or else turn everything back to themselves. Yes, they may express a veneer of empathy for you. But what is happening to you is nothing compared with what they are going through. Or have been through.

The energy vampire leaves us feeling drained and discouraged as they suck out our life force. True friends leave us feeling energized – not the other way around. If you know someone like this, it's time to put in some boundaries. Learn to say 'No' to them, either by starting to put distance between you or simply by not being at their beck and call. If you are worried about what may happen to them, please don't. Once they realize you are no longer available, they will soon find someone else to vampirize.

Parade Rainers
Similar to energy vampires but can be harder to spot. Those who want to bring the rain, bring the pain. People who rain on your parade, either overtly or subtly, undermine your dreams. Unasked, they bombard you with all the reasons why you won't be able to make it. Or they are masters of the art of covert confidence erosion. They seem to be excited for you, and even encouraging. But over time, they begin to drop in demotivational nuggets.

If it's love you're seeking, they will tell you how there are no decent partners left out there. If it's a career change, well, in that area they have thousands of applicants for those positions. Maybe you should rein in those ambitions and save yourself the rejection? If you want to manifest your own business, they've got all the statistics ready to let you know how many fold within the first year. And they only tell you this because they care and don't want to see you fail.

The first thing to remember about the parade rainers is that they are telling their story and not yours. Look at their track record and what they have achieved. Or not, as the case may be. Do they start things but never finish them? Talk about what they intend to achieve but never take any action to make it happen? Do they have their own success stories to share? Recent ones. Not ancient glory days. And stories that are relevant to what you want to achieve? Is this real experience talking or just their opinions?

If you can answer 'No' to even one of these, then this is classic transference. Very often, others rain on our parade out of fear of being left behind. There's a saying: misery loves company. That individual or even a group doesn't want you to change and move away from them. Because if you do, they will be forced to re-examine what they think of as their truth about you, and about what they could potentially achieve. Their inner frenemy can't let that happen. Its very existence is under threat. So, they seek to hold you back and keep you on the same level as them. Rather than let you fly and inspire them instead. Have compassion, but move on.

The second thing to remember is that unless you know 100 percent for certain that the person you're confiding in about your goals is on Team You, the quickest path to successful manifestation is to keep your precious energy for your goals to yourself. And your goals are safe until you have manifested them. This has been a tenet of all major manifestation processes from the very beginning. It's worth repeating: your goals are like tender seedlings. They need protection from the negative elements until they have grown strong roots and fully bloomed.

Sink or Swim? The Sunk Cost Fallacy

The Sunk Cost Fallacy refers to anything we have previously invested in that we are reluctant to let go of – despite the fact it is clearly no longer worth any more of our time, money, or love. This can be as minor as continuing to watch a film we have paid to stream, despite the fact it is boring, all the way up to a relationship we have outgrown or which has become toxic. Instead of stopping the energy drain and reclaiming our power, we find ourselves drowning from the sheer effort of continuing to throw more of our precious resources at it – with no improvement in sight. We continue to invest in it, simply because our mind remains focused on all we have given to it (or the person), in the past, ignoring how much it is now costing us in the present.

The Sunk Cost Fallacy can hold us back from letting go and making room for something better. In financial terms, the saying 'throwing good money after bad' pretty well sums it up. But you can substitute love, friendship, loyalty, support, empathy, and time for the word money and the meaning is just as clear.

If anything is holding you back, then you need to reframe your mind and instead of pouring even more into a friendship that you won't get back, make that empowered choice to invest elsewhere. And please, don't think of this as 'cutting your losses'. You are a dynamic decision maker investing your precious assets elsewhere. Into that incredible future you're in the process of manifesting.

People who need people are the luckiest people in the world. No matter what you are attempting to manifest or achieve, at some point you need people. Yes, right now you may be spending extra time alone working on, say, that bestseller, screenplay, or business plan. But when it's finished, you're going to need that agent, distributor, or backer (and more) to make it all happen. The solo round-the-world sailor needs someone to build their yacht.

Ensure part of your Manifesting Manifesto includes drawing to you the people you need to help and support you. And in the spirit of paying it forward, be prepared to do this to help someone else attain their dream. No, you don't have to be in a position to give someone that Dragons' Den kickstarter. Often all we need is that friend to listen to our plans and who supports us. Whatever role you can play, it connects you to the co-creation factory of limitless success. And what you do for others – know that you can count on them doing that and more for you.

 SUMMARY

Step Six
Embrace Co-Creation Power

- People power! It may sound obvious, but the foolproof way to counteract the negative influence of others is to find someone, or even a group, on your wavelength. And who are magical maverick thinkers themselves. So that they support your freedom and right to go after your dreams. Expand your circle and mix with people on the same vibration. Find a new soul family or community, join my online manifesting community. But people who still value your unique beliefs and individuality. Just as you value theirs.

- Nobody does it alone. It's the one simple truth of manifesting. Even if your dream is to sail solo around the world – you need someone to build your boat. If your desire is to manifest a career as an influencer – you need followers. You may be burning the midnight oil writing that novel – but if you want to be a successful writer you are going to need an agent, a publisher, and, yes, readers. That is why who you know, meet, or are connected to has such an important role in bringing magic into being. People are how the Universe makes the magic manifest.

- Align yourself with your goals and support others as they embark on theirs. Connect with like-minded souls and work together in pursuit of your manifestos. Use the power of group manifesting to superboost your orders. Those we mix with are contagious. So, find others with positive energy and those that inspire you. Get excited about each other's future. The more you energize each other, the faster your orders come in.

- Curate those connections. And stop any madness around feeling you can't rock your authenticity or have to have, be, or do something that goes against that to gain acceptance. If you come to the conclusion that you and another(s) are now on different paths, release them with a loving, universal mindset.

- Do it for others. Speaking your truth and staying true to your heart, you become a limitless warrior of love. When you stand in your truth, you empower others to also create their reality and to follow their path.

STEP SEVEN

LIGHT YOUR SOUL LAMP

Awakening Your Inner Genie

There's a powerful and hidden meaning behind the card of The Hermit in the Tarot. You see a solitary figure holding a lamp of illumination. While the usual interpretation of this card is that of spending time alone and seeking contemplation and solitude, the secret The Hermit is hiding is that they are spending time focusing on what they want to attract into their life. And the light of their lamp is what draws this to them.

Step Seven involves us lighting our soul lamp just like The Hermit. And using its light to draw to us what we desire.

My experience of manifesting is based on the understanding that we are all part of the whole and carry a shard of the divine within us all. Step Six showed us how we are all interconnected on an invisible level. Because we are all interconnected, we are already linked to everything we could possibly desire, so our job is to bring ourselves into alignment on every level and extend our intention toward what we want to draw toward us. That we are all a shard of the divine is our clue that there is nothing external to us to granting our wishes – really, it's us giving it to ourselves.

Each step you take has a ripple effect that impacts the whole. Knowing this connection, you can tap into it by igniting your soul lamp to call in your desires. Lighting up your dreams and visualizing a golden light emanating from within acts as a homing beacon to the cosmos, linking you with the people, coincidences, and circumstances you need to deliver your desires. KNOW that call will be heard and your light will draw what you requested to you.

Have you heard of the mind-blowing scientific phenomenon called quantum entanglement? In a nutshell, it has been proven that when two particles, such as photons or electrons, become entangled, they remain connected even when separated by huge distances. If one changes, no matter how far away the other one is, even if it is across the galaxy, it also changes.

This reveals the interconnectedness of everything. Imagine the Universe as a vast web, with each strand depicting energy, thought, and consciousness. When we focus our intentions on pure belief, we vibrate at a specific frequency on the universal web. Our frequency can then resonate with similar frequencies, attracting experiences and opportunities that align with our desires. Entanglement reveals that our thoughts aren't isolated events but ripples that travel through the web, potentially influencing the fabric of reality itself. Knowing this gives us a stronger ability to hone our belief system and pump up the power of our thoughts.

While the exact way this happens is a scientific mystery, it reminds us that the Universe is interconnected. By aligning ourselves – our thoughts, emotions, and actions – with our true desires, we send out vibrant vibrations that attract our desired reality toward us. So, when we create our Manifesting Manifesto (Step Three), we are entangling ourselves with what we want on a quantum level.

And when we light our soul lamps, we broadcast a homing beacon so that what we want is automatically drawn to us.

Light Your Soul Lamp: Attract What You Desire

I have found this step to be the most potent of all. Every time I have used it, incredible experiences have followed.

Imagine firing up your soul lamp, a radiant flame representing your deepest desires. Feel your whole being radiating shards of golden rays filled with your desires across the Universe. Your flame is the essence of who you are now and who you are capable of being. Your light already knows how to create your future and can magnetize everything you could ever yearn for – the perfect job, fulfilling relationships, a life overflowing with joy – and it already exists as potential within the Universe.

All you need to do is illuminate your own path and watch those desires come radiating toward you.

What You Seek, Seeks You

Here's the secret: you are already part of this vast, interconnected Universe. When you light your soul lamp, its rays aren't simply broadcasting your wishes, they're resonating with the inherent wholeness of everything. Like tuning forks resonating with the same frequency, your desires find a harmonious match within the Universe. It's a calling signal to other like-minded souls and to opportunities.

So, close your eyes and visualize yourself igniting your soul lamp. Feel its warmth spreading within you, filling you with vibrant energy. Remember, your light isn't just about you, it's a beacon that attracts everything and anything that vibrates at

a similar frequency. People who share your values, who resonate with your goals, and who can contribute to creating your
desired reality are drawn toward you now. As are the opportunities, the possessions, the solutions, and all the gifts the cosmos
wishes to bless you with.

As you send out a clear intention along with the glow of your
soul lamp, trust in the Universe's responsiveness. Visualize the
life you desire, the people you wish to meet, the experiences you
crave. Know that the Universe is not just listening but eagerly
aligning with your vibration to effortlessly bring these things
into your life.

Let It Shine!

Like a lighthouse keeper, your dreams can't reach the shore if your
lamp isn't working or is foggy. Purity of intention, unclouded vision,
and unwavering belief are essential to maintaining your lamp.
Keeping your flame bright to attract what you ordered to you.

One of the most effective methods to maintain maximum radiance and ensure our lamplight remains crystal bright and clear
is the simple practice of gratitude.

ACTION STEP

Attraction at the Speed of Life

A common mistake even the most experienced manifestation mages can make is to become so fixated on their goals
that they miss the magic that is surrounding them in the

present moment. Which is why Step Four (Order with the Joy and Expectation of a Child) is so important. It puts us in the miraculous mindset we experienced as a child. Where everything was possible and also when we were totally present in the moment rather than future-projecting to the date we imagined we will finally have what we want and be 'happy'.

By practicing simple gratitude each day, we not only keep our lamps shining at their brightest, we no longer miss the small but beautiful magical blessings that come our way each day. And which act like lodestones on our path.

The more we find to be grateful for, the more we will attract to express gratitude for. And because our minds are now focused on seeking these out, we boost our happiness levels. And reinforce our belief in our abilities to manifest our wildest dreams. And the happier we feel, the more we are in the flow of our lives. And so on. This then turns into a perpetual-motion engine, generating yet more things to be grateful for, more happiness, more flow, and bringing our main manifestation experiences ever closer.

As usual, harnessing the limitless power of the gratitude engine and keeping our lamps burning bright is easy once you know how.

The Power of Three

At the end of each day, list a minimum of three things you have to be grateful for. It's a good idea to jot them down in your journal. This allows you to see just how fast and effective this exercise is.

The beauty of this exercise is that no matter what our circumstances, no matter how many issues we may be grappling with on the way toward manifesting our ideal lives, we can always find three things to list. These can be as simple as a stranger smiling at you or paying you a random compliment. It can be a helpful article or meme you saw online which shifted your mood. It can be sliding into clean sheets when you get into bed. It can be as personal as being grateful for your ability to deal with whatever the day served you. These are your gifts, whether others would consider them significant or not. List them with wholehearted thanks.

You may immediately begin with more than three things to list. Or jump right in with something major to be grateful for. No matter what it is or how many things you have to list, all gratitude is equal. Of course, a big blessing impacts us in a more powerful way than giving thanks for the beautiful cloud formation we saw which inspired and brightened our day. But as far as our lamps and the Universe are concerned, the act of gratitude we engage in for both has exactly the same effect on the cosmos's ability to deliver more to be grateful for. So, don't dismiss the small stuff because it's big stuff when it comes to our blessings.

I love this exercise because it truly can turn from 'a spark to a flame' very quickly. Which is why you need to be writing it down, so you can see how you can go from struggling to come up with three things to easily coming up with so many more to list, within a short time of starting it.

This keeps your flame bright and eternal. It reinforces your belief in your powers of magical manifestor in your life. It connects you to the joy to be found right where you are in the present moment. Which is always where your power resides. Express gratitude for the abundance and happiness that already exist. And in doing so, you'll link to the unshakable surety of what else is heading your way. Let go in peace, trusting your lamp has already set things in motion. Relax, it is all on the way.

 SUMMARY

Step Seven
Light Your Soul Lamp

- What radiates, attracts. Think of your soul lamp as the eternal flame you're lighting that not only symbolizes those desires but acts as the radiance that draws what you want to you.
- Light is energy. By lighting your soul lamp, the energy it sends out entangles with your desires, drawing it to you at the Speed of Life.
- Your light is not just the homing beacon for your goals, it broadcasts the purity of who you really are. It's the essence of your vibration. Your sacred energy. And we know that energetically, like attracts like. So, by sending yours out, clear, unfiltered, and pristine, you automatically begin attracting anything and everything on the same frequency. The people, opportunities, and solutions you've been waiting for will home in on it.
- Gratitude is the fuel that keeps your lamp burning. No matter what our present circumstances, we can always find three things to be grateful for each day. Gratitude glows – but it also grows. As the more we find to be grateful for, the more we have to be grateful for. It's goal acceleration and radiance in one.

PART 3

YOUR MONTHLY MANIFESTING MANUAL BONUS EXERCISES

We've dived into the science, the practical, inspirational techniques of manifesting, but now it's time to put them into action. The power we have to transform our lives is incredible. We are more powerful than we could possibly know. You are a creator and a divine spark of the whole. You now know the powerful steps to take to be a magnet for your desires. Follow the steps and watch your future unfold.

This monthly manifesting course is a bonus, weaving in practical magic to help focus and align your vibration. Of course, the power is always within you. Like Dumbo's magic feather these techniques are an added asset to help you take advantage of practical tools to superboost your manifesting. Like a singer who uses a microphone to amplify their voice, this monthly practice uses the Moon, crystals, vision boards, and exercises to increase your magic. Dive in with all your heart and watch the magic unfold.

Manifesting Journal

Essential to our manifesting month is a manifesting journal. Choose a journal that appeals to you, a journal that entices you and makes you want to pick it up. A book that you feel represents your future. For some folk this might be a tatty exercise book, for others a bejeweled massive and mysterious grimoire. It doesn't matter what you choose as long as every time you look at it you want to pick it up, scribble notes, write down dreams, place sacred orders, paint your future.

Manifesting Month

Although it is best to do this course in order the first time, it is arranged so that in the future you can pick and mix any of the practices to uplift and enhance your manifesting. If you feel you're slipping on the self-love front, dip into that lesson. Fancy being creative? Weave another wishing pouch. If you are ever lost in a sea of doubt, all of these practices can be an anchor back to your power. Plus, many of them, like candle and Moon magic, can be daily or weekly joyful, life-enhancing habits.

At the beginning of your month make a note of the Full and New Moons. These specific energetic wonders will superfuel your practice. Once you have marked the dates in your calendar, look up what sign the New and Full Moons are in and use the Moon guide and manifesting exercise at the end of this chapter.

WEEK ONE

Unique Soul

Nobody has the same goals. Or envisions them in exactly the same form. Yes, many of us may want the same thing – we may want to manifest a loving relationship, abundance, a home, career success. But even if we share a goal with others, it will look just that little bit different for each one of us. After all, you are unique – so it follows that your goals are, too.

Manifesting is therefore a bespoke service. The results are tailored exactly to your order. If we all wanted the same thing – well, it would end up in very short supply and there would be a lot of disappointed people out there! And as we are all unique individuals, what is one person's dream come true could be someone else's 'Where do I get a refund?'

Appreciating our uniqueness, and the individual flavor of our goals, is key to manifesting what's tailored for us. Exquisitely and individually. Unrepeatably unique. But at times we can feel lost and that we have nothing unique to offer. Worse, in the past we may have been lured into adding goals to our list which we thought would enable us to stand out. But which our hearts weren't invested in because they weren't aligned with who we uniquely are. This week's second exercise is designed to remind you of all your unique qualities which you may be overlooking.

If you can, find yourself a nice spot in nature. A garden or park. If this is not possible due to either the weather, time of year, or simply where you live, get yourself a bunch of flowers. If you are outside and there are flowers growing nearby, I'd like you to focus on one. If you are indoors, place the flowers in water and choose one. You may take it and hold it in your hand if you like.

For a few minutes, simply sit and contemplate the absolute perfection and beauty of that flower. Drink in its color. Look at it. Pay attention to it. Begin to notice its details. Even if it's part of a bunch of the same flowers or growing in a bed of similar blossoms, it is subtly and uniquely different from the other blooms. Feel yourself completely understand the flower and almost merge with it, just understanding the magnificence and the miracle of its creation. The arrangement of its petals, its color. Because the longer you look at it, the more you'll see and appreciate all the tiny variations that make it different from the others.

Now, turn this macro-focus on to yourself. Do you now see what a miracle you are? Your divine and beautiful parts which combine in a way that is so fabulously and uniquely you? How come you overlooked all this before? And wasted time trying to be like someone else? Why on earth would anyone do this? This meditation will see you embracing your unique soul.

Now, visualize your heart like a flowering bud. With every breath, imagine it opening up further. Breathe out any desire to imitate others or hurts you've experienced in the past from being made to disown your glory. With every breath in, your authenticity and inner truth open wider. And with every unfolding petal, another layer of beauty and inner power is brilliantly revealed. For as long as you need, bask in the full-bloom fabulousness that is you. Just like the flower, you are radiantly perfect.

Feel that unconditional love for yourself. Unfolding and opening your heart is center to all of your potential. When you are ready, imagine the petals closing to protect your heart as a flower does at dusk. You're now ready to come back into the world again. But now connected to your inner radiance. And all that makes you a brilliant, blossoming soul and the divine miracle that is you.

Remember – our purpose is to evolve the whole through expressing our uniqueness.

Write in your manifesting journal three unique and unusual things you would like to manifest.

Know That It Is Possible – Know That You Deserve It

In Week One it's important to nail the basics. Keep your manifesting journal close and start the first page (or chapter if you have already been using one) and write a LONG list of all the reasons you deserve your manifesting to come in. Write a list of all the wonderful things about you. Write your list as if you were your own best friend. Why do you deserve it?

Next write a list of why it is possible. Write the many ways the Universe might deliver what you desire and the steps you can take to facilitate it. Let your imagination go wild. Of course, the cosmos is always surprising, but opening our heart and mind to wild imaginings helps move us into a place of trust.

The Universe is powerful and will find a way. Who knew my friend would win a competition (she did not know of my manifesting Tobago), and then I ended up sipping rum punch on Pigeon Point Beach with the turquoise waters and meeting magical people who 30 years later are still great friends.

Look back at what has happened that before you thought was impossible? Include coincidences, any dreams in your life that have come true, the return of someone you never thought you'd see again, or a boomerang opportunity you never believed could happen. This just serves as a reminder that nothing is impossible and nothing is out of bounds. You've proved that you can expect the extraordinary as an ordinary outcome of the work you are now doing.

Practical

When I was a single parent with very little money, I used to save up to have a drink in what was then a place called the Hotel Russell (now the Kimpton Hotel). It was in Bloomsbury, London, and I was fascinated by the Bloomsbury set (Virginia Woolf and her fellow members), and by the pre-Raphaelites who lived and worked four minutes from the hotel. Bloomsbury hummed with a creative legacy. I wanted to soak up the glamour and majesty. I would walk into the hotel and take myself to the lost-in-time, marble-clad, leather-seated bar, taking my journal to write poetry and visualize my future. I LOVED doing this.

When I first went, I felt very out of place and self-conscious. But after a few visits I was boldly striding in with my long purple, velvet jacket, ordering my drink and feeling like I was in a home from home. My own private members' club with the spirits of the Pre-Raphs for company. That is the key: changing your energy, matching your energy to where you want to be. Find somewhere that inspires you. Find a place that makes your soul tingle. It could be a crumbling castle that whispers forgotten stories, or Glastonbury steeped in myths and magic. Or an art gallery with all its captured genius. Go where you feel that impossible is now possible, buzz.

Soul Level

We can grasp something on an intellectual level but need to integrate it on an emotional/soul one before we can really put it into practice.

I remember having a big 'Ah-ha!' breakthrough moment. One of the pivotal turning points in my life was when I was heartbroken, exhausted, and struggling. Despite all my manifesting efforts and working them, I felt I had reached breaking point. At rock bottom and with no change in sight, I turned to the Universe and said I had had enough. I did not have the energy to go on, and from the bottom of my soul I poured out my request for help. I desperately wanted to understand how to get to the next step. During that experience, I asked myself some deep questions around whether, if I could manifest anything, then why did I have a block when it came to next level abundance?

If you truly want to know the answer – it will always be given to you. It honestly does work on the same principle as 'ask and you shall receive'. Finally, I realized that what was blocking me was a belief that I had to be the 'perfect' person to attract more money (that old script, I am not good enough). And that I was blocking it until I felt I was one. A pointless and frustrating exercise as of course I would never be 'perfect' enough.

Like a bolt of lightning, I realized that MANY wealthy people are not perfect or even kind. And money itself doesn't make judgments. By the same token, then, why shouldn't kind and empathetic people have financial security too? You can be perfectly kind and empathetic, but that doesn't make you perfect either. Having realized this, from that day forward my attitude toward abundance transformed.

Within weeks, I had been presented with an idea for how to totally turn around my attitude toward receiving abundance. And very soon after, I was moving into a dream thatched cottage with land and horses. This is where our free will and choice come in. When the idea arrived to change my life, I grabbed it with both paws! I was proactive and did not hang around waiting for a lottery win. I knew that the idea was sent to me in answer to my cry for help, and ditching the idea I needed to wait to be 'perfect' before I could experience real abundance was the key to receiving it.

What are your views on abundance and money? What were your parents' views? Are there any hidden beliefs that are stopping the riches the Universe wants to gift you from flooding into your life?

It is important to delve deep on this one as abundance doesn't just include money. It's about being rich in love, time, talent, health, family, friends, and security. What's locked in your vault may be fears and contradictory messages around these. Have you been told you're bad with money, for instance? Do you deep down believe that if you were handed a large sum of money, you'd somehow end up losing it and be broke? If so, this will actively prevent more money from flowing into your life as your core belief is that you not only shouldn't have it, you'll also keep the money away from you to save yourself all the disappointment and unhappiness that losing it (or even having it in the first place) will buy you.

You'll also see how you can substitute any of the other things that make up a life of rich abundance for the word 'money'. So, take some time to make sure you're not putting up barriers between you and what you want to manifest by holding two contradictory beliefs about it at the same time. And know that no matter what it is, perfection is not required for you to have it.

Your Manifesting Manifesto

Words Are Spells, Craft Yours Carefully
One of the most profound truths that changed my ability to manifest was understanding that 'words are spells'. When that sinks in, crafting our future becomes much easier. Our words and thoughts are already weaving what's to come. One of the most powerful tools we have to create our lives are the spells we throw out there every day. Words hold immense power in shaping our experience. Each word we speak shapes our reality, whether aloud or in our thoughts.

It's easy to forget the potency of our language, but how we think and speak about ourselves and others profoundly affects our emotional state and the energy we attract. Paying attention to our words can be transformative. They impact our vibrational frequency, influencing the adventures we draw into our lives. Our constant word spells are what make our manifesto so powerful. We are committing those spells to paper!

In addition to writing an overall manifesto, as in Step Two, practice making mini-manifestos for the weeks and month ahead. What do you want to draw to you this month? What do you want to achieve? Treat these small manifestos as sacredly as you would your main ones. Handwrite them, know it's possible, and use the other steps to make it happen.

WEEK TWO

Harness Your Wonder: Order With the Joy and Expectation of a Child

When we're young, we're all creative. We don't see ourselves as anything else. We don't define and confine 'creativity' to specific areas. It's only later that we encounter the critics who can snuff out our divine spark of creative spontaneity. What we're going to do in your Week Two exercises is reawaken that. And allow ourselves the joy of letting our inner child engage in our manifestation process by expressing itself in creative play. Minus the critical voice.

Manifestation IS creativity. We create a new vision, set of circumstances, a life path, or draw something to us we don't yet have. This is the very definition of creating.

Vision boards have been a mainstream part of the manifesting process for years. I don't believe they are necessary to manifest your desires, but they are fabulous for connecting to our eager, creative inner child. And once we connect with that part of ourselves, then creating magic becomes so much easier. They take our manifesting dreams and bring them into reality. They can be the perfect magical tool to focus, to spin our manifestations into reality. After all, we had an idea and we made the vision board, the next step is already closer.

Although we've seen that writing and doing things with our hands holds extra power, there are many ways to explore vision boards. Yes, there's the traditional take on this of attaching images to an actual board. And if you love the idea of that constant visual reminder hanging somewhere you can't miss it, then this is the option where you can unleash your inner artist and feel the most joy.

But in the digital age we also have other options. You can curate images and create mood boards on Pinterest, where you can set up different boards for each of the things you would like to manifest. Or even have a future life board showing all the kinds of experiences you will have in that future.

Or does a vision journal sound more fun? You can combine words and images, your own illustrations and brightly colored bullet points. There are also vision boards and journaling apps online, which means you can access and update your vision from anywhere, whether you're sitting bored on a train or having coffee in a cafe. Without having to carry a physical notebook around with you. However, do remember that for your initial steps, you MUST use the pen-to-paper method. By all means use apps, but only after you have done the basics old school.

Boards and journals not your thing? Don't worry. You'll discover another tried, true, and creative option later in the section. These exercises are all about playfulness. And they build on the exercises you did last week, strengthening your ties to your knowing that it is possible and that you deserve every single thing on that Manifesting Manifesto declaration.

Joyful, Playful, Hands-on Vision Boarding

There is something enchanting about physically playing with art, to build something from our mind and make it manifest.

I've used vision boarding in my workshops since the early 90s and seeing the sweet joy and excitement as the participants piece together their dreams on paper always inspires me. It never gets old.

You can do this alone or get your friends around to join, inspiring and encouraging each other while having a laugh. Laughter shifts our vibration, lightens us, and helps us step into the right vibration to believe.

How to Capture Your Vision

1. A picture paints a thousand words and also captures moods and energy. Look around to find images that you feel totally represent whatever it is you want to attract. If you want to draw in a relationship, for example, find images of couples sharing the kinds of times you'd like to share with a partner. If you want a holiday, select images of the kinds of places you'd like to visit. Want a new home? Include not only pictures of your dream home but how you'd furnish and decorate it too.
2. You can include single words, quotes, or phrases, such as 'love', 'abundance', or 'I feel great', that pack a powerful emotional punch and reinforce your total faith in what you are envisioning
3. Make the process of putting it all together as magical and immersive as possible. Light candles, put on music that lifts your spirits, and make sure you spend loads of time imagining how amazing your life is going to be as all of this comes in as you put it together. Daydreaming is a powerful state when you can strongly connect with the quantum soup that already contains everything you could possibly want.

All creativity links us to the source – where all that we manifest springs from. It doesn't matter how we express it. What matters is our delight with the process. If you prefer keeping that dream energy under wraps, or simply don't currently have anywhere to display your board, this alternative to vision boarding is another way of tethering your dreams to your joyfulness.

EXERCISE

Bag of Dreams: Create Your Manifesting Pouch

A technique I came up with many years ago and which works just as powerfully as a vision board and potentially even quicker is creating a little bag of dreams I call a magic manifesting pouch. What is a magical pouch? It's a present of the future you receive today. It's like crafting your little bundle of wishes. It's a delightful way to channel your hopes and dreams and connect with your pure spirit of belief that your dreams are on their way.

You can either choose to make your own manifesting pouch or buy a ready-made one. The one condition is that you love the fabric. Choose a color, texture, or pattern that evokes a sense of beauty and inspiration. Something vibrant, captivating, and what you feel is aligned with and embodies the energy of your goals. After all, it's going to wrap them with all your precious visions for your future. Not just any old scrap.

Of course, your choice could be plain black or white. And there's nothing wrong with that. Black is the color of the void and the Great Attractor. Where all that will come into being in this Universe resides according to many cultures. Amazingly, white light is a combination of all the colors of the rainbow and is a great blank slate to draw your wishes. What matters is not the color but whether it speaks to your soul.

Next, gather up your treasures. The small items you have chosen to represent your desires. These can be symbolic but also deeply meaningful. The connection may be obvious or more esoteric. What matters is its significance to YOU.

Perhaps one of your goals is a bucket-list trip, for instance. So you may include a feather to symbolize getting on that aircraft and taking off to your dream. Or a seashell represents that beach house. A key could represent unlocking anything from that front door to someone's heart – or your own talent vault. Or perhaps there's someone whose qualities you admire and wish to emulate? Why not include a photograph of them to act as inspiration? You can also include pictures of anything you specifically wish to manifest. From that car to that dream wedding dress.

Crystals are another key addition to your pouch. Because you can choose a crystal companion to your other items which is associated with a specific area, emotional state, or healing quality you are going to need. You may choose rose quartz to beckon love or boost your self-love, tiger's eye for strength and courage, or pyrite for abundance. Clear quartz points are like mini-magic wands and are brilliant to enhance all manifesting.

You can add a sprinkle of herbs, such as dried sage for protection and to hold the energy, or rosemary for clarity. This is your creation, so craft your little bundle of wishes. If you are making your own pouch, don't forget to choose some ribbon or cord to go with it.

Now you have gathered your magical blend of ingredients, time to infuse them together. If you are using your own fabric, you can choose a no-sew option by cutting it into a square. The sewers among you can, of course, choose to stitch their pouch on a machine, speaking your desires into each stitch. But no matter whether you opt for creating your own or buying a pre-made pouch, this does not affect how it works.

First, cleanse your crystal. Run it under water. If it's a wand then point it down, hold it in your right hand, and say something like, 'I dedicate you to my good and the good of all'. Still holding it in your right hand, think about a chosen goal. Infuse your crystal with your intention. See it happening, feel excited at the prospect, and secure in your belief that it can and will manifest. Now, write down this particular goal on a piece of paper. This is your order form.

Next, wrap the crystal in your written order. As you enclose it, repeat your order like a mantra. Feel the anticipation bubbling within you as you call your desire into being. Place your wrapped crystal into your pouch. Or at the center of your fabric square if you are creating your own and using the no-sew technique.

With this include herbs and any other talismans you've chosen. Think of this as a present to yourself. Because guess what? You're about to receive this gift in real form when your desires come knocking. Fold over the fabric to enclose all your items and tie it up with your ribbon or string. Now choose a special, sacred, and undisturbed spot to store your magical pouch. Know that even if it is out of sight, it is constantly working like a magnetic treasure chest to draw your dreams to you.

Need a bigger bag for those dreams? Or an entire set of dream luggage? You can create as many pouches as you like. One for each goal you have. Or pack all your goals into one gorgeous, glorious pouch of dreams.

Because every part of the seven steps and the exercises are all about empowerment and personal choice, and aligning your energy to your personal goals and dreams, some of you may be more inspired by the magical pouch exercise than by creating a vision board. You can choose one or you can do both. It's about what works for you. But both work equally well.

WEEK THREE

Back to Your Future Self

Week Three is the perfect time to reconnect to Future You. Think of this like meeting for a catch-up with a close friend you haven't seen in a couple of weeks. A lot has happened! And because you and Future You are co-creators and cosmically entangled, it means that changes which may already be occurring within you have already influenced Future You. And vice versa. As usual, turn off your phone and find a comfy space where you won't be disturbed. Your future deserves the focus and quality time you'd give to a friend.

Close your eyes and imagine you are seated in a cinema and waiting for the film to begin. Glance around and take in who is in the audience – especially those sitting closest to you. Do you know them already? If not, do you 'feel' you know them on some level? Pay special attention to them if so. Take note of their appearance, how they are dressed, and your general overall impression of them. What does this tell you about who they are? What do they do? If you don't recognize them (yet), what role do you think they may have to play in your future?

As the lights go down and the screen comes to life, imagine you're watching a real-life scene one year into your future. Where are you? Who are you with? What do you look like? Has your appearance changed? Are the people you are with in your life now, or have you yet to meet them? Spend as much time as you need and 'follow' your future self around for however long it takes. Allow the scene or several scenes to unfold.

Does Future You have something to say to you? A speech to make? A revelation to share? Do they take you somewhere unexpected? Have they undergone an emotional arc or transformation? If so, how has this affected the storyline? Be willing to allow the script to take you where it needs to go. Remember, this is a co-production between you and your future self. So allow it to unfold as it needs to without feeling the need to step in and begin directing it.

When you are ready, return your conscious focus to your seat in the audience.

Look around at how the audience has reacted to the 'performance'. What are they saying? Who is saying it? Get your journal out and write down as many details as you can about what you have seen. Both on-screen and off. From your impressions of the people who surround you and their responses. To your own take on what was happening on screen. Did something surprise you? Inspire you? Could you have predicted what would happen? Or did the storyline veer off in an exciting new direction you hadn't thought of but are now intrigued to explore?

Did your on-screen Future Self have an important message for you? Had they achieved more than you imagined for yourself? If so, know now that you can too!

The great thing is, you only have to wait 12 months to verify this. Very often, when we see a future that excites us, we start to prepare for it. Our energy levels rise and we make changes, for instance to our appearance, so it matches what we have seen, bringing the future to us much faster. If what you see concerns you, please don't worry. To quote Hermetic wisdom,

'The All is Mind; the Universe is Mental.' Or to paraphrase Yoda from the film *The Empire Strikes Back*: always moving about is the future.

What you've seen is a gift, as you have the power to change your future experience. If you begin to do this and repeat the exercise in a month or so, watching the box set of your life, I guarantee you will be shown something very different. Like all good movie franchises, you can always expect a sequel!

Group Power

Groups are power, they influence us in ways beyond our understanding. You may have to disconnect from a group in order to believe in the possibilities that exist for you, for instance. And find a new loving and supportive community. You need to understand that what may be true for the group, may not be your truth. No matter what, embarking on a manifesting journey will deliver you one key truth: people matter. They will turn out to be your greatest resource. They are your co-creators and collaborators in making the magic happen. Even if they appear only at the very end stages. (Remember what I said about sheltering those dreams until they have firmly taken root and flowered.)

Keep in mind the beautiful flower meditation you did as part of your Unique Soul work of Week Two. Because this illustrates brilliantly how we can bloom in our own way, appreciate our individual traits, but also be part of a bunch. In other words, you are part of the great creative collective that is made up of the souls on the planet. But you are not lost in it, nor do you feel any pressure to be unduly influenced by it.

Group Manifesting – Creating With Your Bunch

Perhaps you've experimented with role-playing in relationships, where you pretend to meet for the first time in a bar, adopting new personas and flirting with each other? This is great fun and can allow partners to let go in a way they might not usually. It's permission to express your desires without any hangups. Now, consider manifesting role-play! Gather your friends (or suggest it in an online manifesting group where you can do this entirely online) and arrive as your future selves.

You can do this over dinner, lunch, or a picnic in the park. Set a date one, five, or ten years in the future, imagining you haven't seen each other in that time. Excitedly share your accomplishments and the fulfilling lives you've created. The key is to be genuinely enthusiastic for each other's success.

What is fascinating about this practice is that you will probably uncover details of things that make you happy that you didn't even know. It gives you freedom to explore what your future will look like in ways that will surprise and delight you. Talk about your lover, your home, what you've accomplished creatively. The joyful adventures you've had and how you've grown within yourself. Not only is this powerful group work, but there's a sprinkle of sugar from your future self whispering the wonder of what's to come for you.

WEEK FOUR

Light Your Soul Lamp

By lighting and polishing your soul lamp your inner genie can get to work on connecting you to what you want. Your dreams aren't just fantasies but glimpses into your potential future. In another dimension, you may already be living those dreams: practicing yoga in Bali, signing copies of your bestselling novel, strolling through the woods of your sustainable home, enjoying a fulfilling date with your perfect partner. Essentially, your dreams are yours to claim. The more we light our soul lamp and feel rays of our desires spread across the Universe, KNOWING that we can draw toward us all the coincidences, people, and opportunities we need to make it happen, the brighter our light becomes and the quicker we manifest.

Regularly create the space to do this. You can do it in the bath when you are relaxed, or while taking a walk. The time just before nodding off to sleep is highly potent. You might even find clues to the next steps in your dreams.

Visualize every pore of your being filled with the creator light that is unique to you, your very own shard of the divine. Feel the light radiating from you in all directions, like you're a disco glitter ball of intention. Feel yourself living, breathing, and experiencing what you want to manifest. It's familiar to you as it is your reality. Feel utterly refreshed and excited for the future that you know you deserve and believe is possible.

Manifest Your Desires With Quantum Entanglement (Soul Lamp Two)

Another way to light your lamp is to get frisky with quantum entanglement.

Quantum Entanglement: A Reminder

Imagine two particles, even far apart on opposite sides of the Universe, connected and instantly influencing each other. Change one and the other changes too. It's a bit mind-bending, but it suggests a powerful connection at the very foundation of reality.

Think of reality as a vast, responsive energy field. Your thoughts and feelings, especially strong emotions, create vibrations within this field. Focusing on what you lack only amplifies that lack. But we can 'link' positive emotions we've already experienced with our future desires through quantum entanglement.

The Quantum Entanglement Technique

1. **Find Your Calm:** Choose a quiet time and place. Relax, close your eyes, and take some deep breaths.
2. **Choose Your Focus:** What do you deeply desire? More money? A loving relationship? Pick one area to start.
3. **Recall and Relive:** Think back to a time in the past when things were good in this area, even in a small way. Remember the joy, abundance, or love you felt. Let those feelings fill you up.
4. **Entangle!** Holding those positive feelings, visualize your desire fulfilled. Imagine your ideal life in vivid detail and the amazing emotions you'll experience. Merge this future vision with the joyful memories of your past.

How the Magic Happens

This technique goes beyond visualizing. You're creating a powerful energetic entangled link between the good feelings you've known and the even better things you desire. This shift in your vibration tells the Universe what to bring your way. And whenever doubts try to sneak in, you can revisit those positive feelings to stay aligned with your goal.

Lantern Manifesting Abundance

When you're manifesting, you're transcending ordinary reality, entering a realm of infinite abundance. Instead of trying to mold the Universe to fit your limited perception, you must expand your mind to embrace limitless possibilities. That's why, when manifesting, it's more powerful to set intentions that leave the details to the Universe. This creates a magical space where unexpected wonders can flow into your life.

You are the architect of your own experience and you get to choose how to build it. If you're working on manifesting a new career, for instance, consider the difference between saying, 'I want a job with X company at X salary with X hours where I get to do X' and saying, Okay Universe, show me what's possible!'

So, whenever you're setting an intention, ask yourself: 'Am I limiting myself or am I opening doors to new possibilities?'

You can start small or go large with this one. However, step one is all about knowing it is possible and that you deserve it. I recommend the first time you try it that you only go as far as you KNOW is possible. Keeping in mind the Universe is very happy to surprise you if you let it.

Buy a lantern as a visual representation of your soul lamp. Every time you light the lantern, see the rays of your desires spreading throughout the Universe drawing, to you all the people, experiences, and coincidences you need to manifest your chosen destiny.

BONUS TIP

Candles as Manifesting Machines

Every time I light a candle in my home, for a dinner party, for ambient lighting, or any reason at all, I always make a wish, put a circle of love around my home, or send blessings to one of my family members. Try it, it works!

EXERCISE

Once a Week – Your Day Off to Dream

Hey, daydream believer! Are you sitting at home thinking, 'Oh my god, I am lovesick, I am pining, I am pining, bring me the love now'? Or are you waiting for that cash infusion? Whatever you've ordered, I want you to do something for me today: I want you to let it go. And as ironic as that sounds, that is the very thing that could bring your order to you, boom! Just like that.

Because the paradox is, the tighter you grasp it, the more out of reach it becomes. And when you bombard that goal with all your energy, that's not focus. That's desperation. We've discussed how you need to order with the joy and expectation of a child in Step Three.

Hanging on for dear life, directing every waking moment into wondering when your order will be fulfilled also negates all that work you did in Step Two – knowing it is possible. Because this now says you doubt it is. Otherwise you wouldn't be feeding that fear that this is all taking too long. You'd be flowing with total trust and knowledge that the Universe is colluding in your favor.

As I said earlier, it's exactly like ordering something from Amazon or Deliveroo. You order it and you let it go. You don't keep checking up on it. (Okay, if you're starving you may keep checking how far off that pizza is. But you know what I mean.) You have no doubt, however, that it is on its way. You are relaxed about it.

Let Go to Attract What You Want

Which is why this once-a-week practice is important. So just for today, forget your order, no matter how much you want it, how much it hurts, how much you're longing for that message or call, that solution, or that payment to show up in your bank account. For now, you're going to let it go and do something fabulously alternative with your day. And rebuild your trust with the Universe. Because otherwise, you actually haven't sent out your Manifesting Manifesto at all. It's like an email stuck in your outbox because you forgot to press 'Send'. The network's down. You haven't let it go.

What Is for You Cannot Pass You by

Remember the lesson of waiting for the future to appear? The time when we reach our goal? The trap of waiting for that moment to gift ourselves with happiness which prevents us from all the magic that surrounds us in the 'present'? This exercise not only restores our belief that our goal is possible, it allows us to live a version of the dream we are creating for ourselves right NOW.

And yes, dropping that obsessive phone checking, energy bombardment, and constant refreshing of that inbox won't mean you'll miss out. Because what is meant for us can never pass us by. This tells you: now I can relax.

So, surrender today, have a fabulous time doing something that you adore. It's play time! This could be something you've always enjoyed, way before you even began your manifesting journey. That side hustle which feels like pleasure. That thing you've been promising yourself you would do but keep putting off. That part of town with the intriguing shops or restaurants you want to check out. That tai chi class that's scheduled for today. That art gallery. Or just the outdoors that's calling you. That park, that canal path, that beach, that wild place that inspires your soul.

All that matters is that it captures your attention, brings you back to your bliss – and unplugs you from energy bombing those goals. You've done so much miraculous work on your manifesting path – don't you think you've earned some time off? Reset and restore your faith in what's possible and live a present-moment version of your future dream today. And let go of the dream to take care of itself.

The Free Manifesting Power of the Moons

Every month there is a New and a Full Moon which radiate possibility. Tuning in and using the Moons is a cosmic cheat sheet to your goals. Each Moon offers a different gift. So whenever you start your month, drop in an order for that Moon's vibe.

New Moons allow us to release and shed past energy, to cast out anything or anyone we no longer want. New Moons are also wishing Moons and are especially good for new starts and planting the seeds of our desires. They are a portal of possibility, a bubbling, energetic cauldron mixing the right elements to bring us to our dreams. Part of that is our ability to let go, to allow something more right for us to enter.

Full Moons are peak experiences. As we head toward the Full Moon, our energy builds. Full Moons are known to be very emotional, but with our new-found manifesting skills we can use that peak to our advantage.

One word of warning: it is not advisable to manifest on an eclipse as they are chaotic and can create dodgy consequences. Eclipses are all about hiding things. When we manifest during an eclipse, we might not be clear about the consequences. Use eclipses as time off and wait for the energy to pass.

How to Use the Moons in Your Monthly Practice

So how do we use the magical Moons in our monthly practice? Download a free Moon app or look online (you can look at your monthly astrology on my website to see the Moons of the month: horoscope.co.uk) and find out the date and sign of the New and Full Moons for the month. Have fun with this. Use the Moons for bonus orders. Then check out the Moon manifesting catalogue and decide what you want to order!

ARIES

New Moon

Aries is the first sign in the zodiac so has unique magic. Fearless Aries brings courage, impulsiveness, and va va va voom – and the energy of being a hero for yourself. Bold and free, the Aries New Moon helps manifest confidence, self-assurance, and the bravery to enter into a new path with enthusiasm and zest. Ditch other people's opinions or self-doubt and use this Moon to forge your authentic path. Aries is a fire sign that releases our doubts. Just before the New Moon, write down your fears on a piece of paper and then burn and surrender them. (Safety first: if you can't do this in a garden, use a fireproof dish in the sink.) On the New Moon write a short bullet-point (Aries likes to cut to the chase) Manifesting Manifesto on what daring things you want to manifest in the next month, year, and lifetime. Like Aries, don't worry about the details, write it down and it is done! Oh, and Aries is immediate-action energy, so take one exciting step toward what you want to achieve.

Full Moon

The fiery, passionate, and independent Full Moon in Aries brings a surge of eager and willful energy. It's a peak experience of impulse, power, and fearlessness. What can you use this huge energy for? Where in your life could you benefit and move forward by having the daringness to do so? What would you say if you had the nerve? How would that transform your life? This Full Moon can help you with that. Once the Full Moon in Aries

163

passes (the Moon then moves into stable Taurus); it's important to ground yourself, keeping inside the courage that the Aries Full Moon has unlocked.

This is also a Full Moon of utter and total acceptance. Embrace who you are with fearless and unapologetic intent. Rekindle that self-belief and also relink to Step Two (Know It Is Possible and Know You Deserve It) and Step Four (Order With the Joy and Expectation of a Child) if needed.

If you find yourself alone under this Full Moon, be happy with your own company. Don't seek love in all the wrong places – especially if inner you is saying it doesn't feel right. You are enough for you and flying solo under this Full Moon means you get to appreciate all you are, all over again. Above all, consciously steer clear of negative thoughts around relationships or loneliness. Especially anything around love passing you by or that there are no 'good' ones out there. This Full Moon asks you to acknowledge you are on your way to getting whatever you set out to manifest. Look and you will find your progress. And also that no matter what beliefs you have held in the past, you are not missing out on anything. It is on its way.

TAURUS

New Moon

Taurus is an earth sign that represents sensuality, security, and abundance. Loyal, dependable, and stubborn, the Taurus New Moon allows us to release any patterns, circumstances, or people that destabilize us. What do sensuality and security look like to you? What do you want to manifest in these areas? Common things to manifest with earthy Taurus include feeling secure in your body, not only accepting yourself but embracing the wonder of your physical form. Taurus is ruled by Venus, the planet of love and abundance, so committed relationships and sensual ones are available to order. (Remember, it is not cool to mess with someone else's life path, so be general when you do this – no matter how tempting, no naming names! Although you can request security within your family. That will unfold for the good of all. Manifesting a new home, a better environment, and an increase in abundance.)

This New Moon asks you if you know your true worth. Also linked to this is what you believe 'rich' is. As well as those goals around security and abundance, you get to look at your values (including how you value yourself) and those hidden emotional 'riches' – relationships. A rich inner life is the priceless takeout we all deserve and desire. Without it, the outer stuff gets pretty meaningless. So, include the precious and intangible assets of self-love and riches of contentment, support, and sensuality too. This New Moon also unlocks your creativity and appreciation for the arts. Add music as your muse as you vision board, write, journal, or paint. If you are seeking love at the time of this New Moon, become your own lover first.

Full Moon

How are you showing up for yourself? If you were reliable and grounded, what would reaching a peak of that energy look like? We climb toward a Full Moon, it is a summit moment. What sensual, abundant, or home heights can you visualize and know are possible? It's also the perfect time to celebrate your blessings. To honor the stable people and forces in your life. Surround yourself with the people you love; have a cosy night knowing that comfort is increasing. If you are in the Southern Hemisphere, make a feast of your favorite foods and have a picnic under a tree. If you are in the Northern Hemisphere, indulge in the Danish practice of Hygge where you retreat into a space of snuggly things that make you feel safe and content while visualizing the ultimate heartwarming experiences to come.

Take advantage of Venus energy to massage yourself (or a lover) with rose or sandalwood oil, and connect with Venus. Ask her to deliver the love and abundance you desire. This is a Full Moon of appreciation, asking us to slow down, become less competitive, and simply more appreciative of what we have right now. Remember our gratitude exercise? There's no better Full Moon under which to take out your journal and look at just how much you have had to be grateful for in the weeks or months leading up to this Full Moon. Far, far more than you probably imagined or remember. In doing so, you will be planting even more seeds for abundant growth. This Full Moon reminds you: you're richer than you think.

GEMINI

New Moon

The charming Gemini New Moon brings the gift of a quick wit, communication, curiosity, and a dash of inspiration. Having problems expressing your ideas? Blocked from speaking your truth? Throw your fears into the Gemini New Moon vortex. KNOW that you can access your voice. Want to write that novel, reboot your online presence, bring that idea into reality? The Gemini New Moon amplifies your mind. Open your manifesting journal and without thinking about it too much write a free-flowing list of ideas and inspirations. Write down everything without editing or judging the thoughts that come through. When you've finished, take a break, listen to or read something that stirs your creativity, then go back to your writing and see which parts you want to build on and take forward. It might be a list of concepts for a book, a course, or ways in which you can make your brilliance known. Visualize the future where you have succeeded in expressing yourself in a concrete way.

But don't forget – talk is cheap and actions speak louder than words. It's this and the quality of your words that matter now. Because of this, don't scatter that precious genius, which is what can happen under a Gemini Moon. It can deliver so many ideas, choices, and options that we become over-enchanted with the mere concept of them and so end up just talking a great game rather than bringing it. Even if you just have one hero concept that excites you right now, it's a great time to reread the part about focus – and get laser precise about how you apply it. And yes, of course, serve this with follow-through. Words and ideas are your spells. Action is what sets the spell in motion.

Full Moon

Be prepared for a frenzy of activity, social interactions, messages, and a head full of buzzing ideas. The Full Moon in Gemini is a perfect time to change direction and pivot toward what truly inspires you. (Warning: if you aren't channeling your thoughts, you could end up being argumentative.) Channel the energy for win/win solutions. If you've been manifesting a proposal, now is the time to put it out there. Pitches, applications, and submissions – this is their launch window. Time to send them winging their way out there.

Have something to say but been hesitating over saying it? Or simply struggling to find the right words? This Full Moon brings a need to say it anyway and an upswell of the pitch-perfect ways to convey it. Or if you have been struggling to find your unique voice, the Gemini Full Moon tells you that you have one – and shows you how to use it.

Mercury-ruled Gemini can bring instant solutions. Grab your journal and write down a problem or block you have. Now immediately start writing the solution. Full Moons drag up thoughts and feelings that come from our unconscious. This technique can not only connect with the sharpest Mercury messages but highlights any negative thoughts getting in your way. Write the solutions and then rewrite your affirmations.

CANCER

New Moon

Cancer is the sign of nurturing, home, and family. The crab needs to feel secure, so the New Moon in Cancer is the perfect time to release family blocks or insecurities. The New Moon in Cancer allows us to lay down a secure foundation for our future. It gives us something to 'hold on to'. It's perfect for manifesting house moves, career progression, and creating a solid foundation from which you can launch yourself or your plans into the big wide world. It offers you an opportunity to surrender patterns, habits, and beliefs that no longer serve you. How can you support yourself to feel more secure and protected?

What do you believe your future holds in terms of home and family? Get excited about what is possible.

Use the Moon to honor your precious spirit, offer yourself love and acceptance. Cast out your dreams for the future, knowing it is possible. Harness the Moon's energy to honor your inner strength and worth. Embrace your dreams with confidence, knowing they are achievable and inevitable. Create a vision/Pinterest board for your home and do delicious, cosy things today.

Full Moon

Water Full Moons can be very emotional. Our vulnerability rises to the surface on the tides of La Luna. While this might feel uncomfortable, great strength can be harvested from our vulnerability. Being vulnerable is one of our primal fears and many of us will do anything to avoid it. How we relate to our own vulnerability is hugely important in terms of who we are and how we live, however. Masking how we feel to avoid being hurt, rejected, or made to feel ashamed can push us to living our lives one step away from where the authentic action is. It also sets up a vibration of fear that means the Universe cannot deliver what we really want.

There's a huge difference between taking a risk and being reckless. The same kind of difference there is between plucking up the courage to tell someone how much they mean to us and swearing at the boss who has annoyed us. It's also about walking a delicate line between expressing our feelings yet still taking responsibility for them. Being vulnerable means admitting when we're afraid, sad, or scared. But not expecting anyone to rescue us. It's about emotional ownership. Strengths, vulnerabilities, warts and all. Being true to our authentic selves and allowing others to be true to their authentic selves.

When we are in our power, we know that no matter what happens or what anyone does, nothing can erode or diminish that part of us that is sacred and eternal. Use this Moon to explore your vulnerability. Take out your journal and write down one area where you're feeling vulnerable and then list ways in which you can express it and heal.

Before the night of the Full Moon:

1. Buy and cleanse a moonstone crystal, leaving it to charge in the moonlight for a night or two. (If you don't have one, a clear quartz will do.)

2. As you do this, focus on its association with emotional balance and nurturing energy.
3. Gather soft, fluffy towels and calming essential oils (like lavender or chamomile), and set the ambiance in your bathroom with candles and your fave chill-out music.

The ritual:

1. On the night of the Full Moon, prepare a luxurious bath that makes you feel truly pampered.
2. Add the essential oils and perhaps white rose petals for an indulgent touch.
3. Slip into the warm water, holding the moonstone in your left receiving hand.
4. Close your eyes and envision the moonlight flowing into the water, infusing it with lunar energy.

As you soak, reflect on the feeling of security and nurturing you long for. Let any tension wash away. Visualize this sense of wellbeing growing stronger, surrounding you like a comforting cloak. Know that you are manifesting an abundance of nurturing energy in your life.

LEO

New Moon

What's outside your comfort zone? You might think, 'Here be dragons!' But the reality is that outside your comfort zone is where the magic happens. It's where our lives change, new possibilities enter, and we can live a more fulfilling life.

Most of us know all this and yet we hesitate or tie ourselves into knots of fear at the mere thought of leaving the safety of what's familiar and secure. This can be for many reasons. Perhaps we have been made to think we are not good enough, that we will fail, that we will look stupid, or meet with rejection and ridicule. But the good news is that change can be easier than you think, and the Leo New Moon is here to help.

This feisty Moon urges us to ditch whatever is stopping us from standing in our radiant power. To face the dragon head on. It gives us that extra oomph of confidence and a sprinkle of 'Look at me!' energy. It hands you permission to take a risk to stride confidently out into the world. It's also loaded with luck. How will you choose to take a chance?

Remember, you have a unique voice the world needs to hear. Use the Leo New Moon to consciously cast out your fears. Think of what you would do if you dared. Now write it in your manifesting journal as something you are ready to receive.

Full Moon

Channel Your Inner Brave

The Full Moon in Leo can bring a peak of confidence. Confidence is a powerful seasoning to our manifesting sauce. Sometimes, we feel more fearful than brave, but you're stronger than you think and the Leo Full Moon is available for you to call that fearlessness down.

The Universe rewards bold moves. What would you do today if you were brave, courageous, and confident? Let this Leo Full Moon give you a boost of courage, even if it's just taking a tiny, brave step.

Strut With Confidence

We all have wobbly moments, but remember, you are fabulous! Channel that Leo energy and work that confident walk. The real confidence will follow even if you have to fake it initially. This sends a clear signal to the Universe about what you claim for yourself. I learned this firsthand from a woman called Racine Ripple whom I met in the 1980s. I was fascinated by her as a room stopped whenever she walked in. Racine was a Leo and as she walked, a huge cloud of charisma surrounded her. I noticed that she had a different energy from anyone I knew and I craved that confidence.

I was 15 and a little lost punk who lived in a women's squat in Brixton. She took the time to share with me to 'act as if' and to visualize my confidence. Her wisdom had a profound impact on me. I immediately took her advice and it worked! Sadly, Racine passed away quite young, but her kindness and wisdom changed my life, a living embodiment of the 'ripple effect', and I shall never forget her.

What makes your heart sing? This Leo Full Moon is about putting your desires front and center. Set your sights high and take a small, practical step in that direction today. Maybe it's sketching out those big ideas in a soul map or writing your Manifesting Manifesto, which focuses on success.

Celebrate Your Wins

Leos love parties. Don't underestimate the power of celebration. The Full Moon reminds us to acknowledge all we've created and overcome. Big or small, give yourself a pat on the back. Maybe it's a special treat, a dance party in the living room, or sharing your successes with a supportive friend. Celebrate YOU!

Gratitude Glow-Up

When we focus on gratitude, we amplify abundance. Take some time to list all the things you're grateful for. This doesn't have to be major stuff as we've already talked about – the warm sunshine, the perfect cup of coffee, the friend who always makes you laugh. This positive energy attracts even more soul-glow goodness.

VIRGO

New Moon

Perform an act of devotion to something new under the detail-focused New Moon in Virgo. Virgo is the sign that says you don't need 'it all'. You only need what is right for you. The New Moon in Virgo gives us super-pristine focus. We take care of the details and can hone into exactly how to achieve our desire. We don't sweat the small stuff. And we suddenly see – it's all small stuff. What we imagined was daunting gets cut down to bite-sized pieces.

Declutter your orders: How many orders have you sent to the cosmos? Run through your manifesting journal, manifesto, and vision boards. Delete anything you have outgrown. Carrying around desires we no longer want can scatter our energy. If we aren't 100 percent into it, we are wasting our time and our energetic resources.

Place a single order and give it your full focus. Hone onto one thing that you want and using the steps, concentrate all of your energy on that one precious order. Which order can you choose that you KNOW you are ready for right now?

Rituals of Service: Consider simple acts of service that improve your environment or help another. We are all deeply connected to the whole and by helping others we are in fact supporting ourselves. Our responsibility (Virgo is all about responsibility) is to add healing and wonder to the world. To reach out and help others achieve their goals too. When we do this with an honest heart, we not only benefit from a dopamine hit, we also uplift our vibration. Virgo magic is also telling you it is incredibly important to look after yourself. By taking care of you, you reinforce to the cosmos that you know you are worthy. How is your self-care right now? Release patterns that no longer serve you.

Full Moon

Details are everything. Devotion to them, the secret ingredient to success. And your gateway to making everyday magic happen.

Look out for a dream, synchronicity, or message delivered by the practical Virgo Moon. Virgo is all about the details, so expect a message about how a small detail change can speed up your order. Ruled by Mercury, if you are seeking answers, now is the time to ask for them. Especially in a specific area. Know that you WILL receive your answer, but under this insightful yet pragmatic Full Moon, it will be what you need to know – not necessarily what you want to hear. Do be open to what you are told, and the adjustments you may need to make to enact its wisdom. Keep in mind, these are for your ultimate wellbeing and are designed to clear the path toward your goals.

Be grateful – Virgo's truth asks for a detailed gratitude practice appreciating life's small wins. Paying attention to the tiny details increases the big stuff. The more you foster a vibe of appreciation, the higher your vibration.

Go within – Virgo vibes help us detox our habits and patterns. Virgo is an earth sign, so use nature as a superboost to a Virgo Full Moon. Look at what you need to release. See this as clearing the space for something healthier to manifest. Even in a city, we can find nature. And use it to supercharge our intentions. Write down one thing that no longer supports or serves you. That routine which has turned into a rut, a self-soothing habit which does you no good, that procrastination which is actually fear in disguise. Then write down something healthier, enlivening, and energizing that would have the space to manifest once you released the old toxic pattern. Slip out into nature and place it under a tree. Feel your energy ground. And what you want to let go of, harmlessly disperse into the earth. Know that as the tree grows, so does your wish as new habits and daily miracles take root.

LIBRA

New Moon

A Time of Manifesting Magic, Love, Romance, and All Things Beautiful

Libra is ruled by Venus, the planet of love and abundance, so this New Moon is exceptional for inviting love into our lives. Lovely Libra is the perfect Moon to manifest all things relationship related plus abundance (Venus rules money and possessions and the good things of life).

It is about harmony, beauty, and restoring balance. Luna Libra wants you to know you are treasured. If you don't feel cherished, then this is the Moon to sort it out. It's an invitation to conjure peace. What do you want to surrender and what is no longer serving you in these areas? Look to this, so that balance and harmony can be your default setting once more.

Libra is the sign of partnerships. The divine balancing act and dance. The symbol of the scales, which are equal when we are relating to ourselves in a balanced and harmonious way. All our outer relationships reflect the one we have with ourselves. This New Moon not only invites you to explore that but also to see yourself in a new light. This is one of the most magnetic New Moons of the year. Where we can attract people, opportunities, and new things to 'relate' to. Remember, all manifestation comes from interaction and our relationship to ourselves and then the Universe. When we relate, we automatically open up to attract.

Write a little personal audit on how balanced different sections of your life are. Where do you feel you're missing out? Include time for yourself, loving moments, work, how much time you spend online, etc. Visualize yourself in the future where you have gorgeous balance, the love you deserve, plus you're thriving in harmony with yourself.

Full Moon

Manifest Romance, Love, and Justice

As the Full Moon in Libra approaches, you have the power to experience its magic. A time of manifesting romance, love, and justice. So take control, set your intentions, and feel the energy rising.

Full Moons draw things from our unconscious and bring what is happening to our awareness. It's the full emotional experience. Expect a nudge and a message from the magical Moon rays on what needs to shift to bring you the balance you need. Approaching the world with a heart filled with love has the power to shift and transform our experiences in all situations. Yes, it's challenging, especially when we feel wronged or life doesn't offer what we believe we deserve. Yet, remember that at our core, we are beings of love.

This Full Moon can open a portal for you to release those old patterns. It shows you where you have blindly been on a rinse-and-repeat cycle. Doing something and getting the same result. Even if the wrapper looked different – it turned out to be the same chocolate each time! Now the blinders come off. There's a link to the card of Justice in the Tarot under this Full Moon and meditating on it can help with this. This Full Moon is often another pivot point on our manifestation journey as it exposes what we have been repeating. So we repeat it no more. And then watch, awestruck, as something different and exciting is attracted in effortlessly as a result. It also hands us the compassion we need to show ourselves rather than self-blame for becoming trapped by what no longer works.

Just for today, try putting on your love-tinted glasses. See the world through a lens of compassion, kindness, and understanding. Instead of focusing on hurt or a sense of lack, seek the good in others and the blessings within your life. You may be amazed at how the world transforms right before your eyes.

SCORPIO

New Moon

Rising From the Flames. Letting Go. Rebirth

Scorpio is symbolized by not only the scorpion but also the eagle and the phoenix. This potent and primal Moon helps manifest total transformation. Scorpio, ruled by Pluto (and also Mars), is famous for endings, death, and rebirth.

This New Moon is your gift if you want to end a cycle, relationship, or pattern. Scorpios are not afraid to get down and dirty. There's a survival instinct in Scorpio that you can tune into now. They are the psychic detectives of the zodiac and can sniff out a lie from 100 miles away. You can shed jealousy, secrets, and shadows, release them into the dark hole of the Scorpio New Moon, and rise like the phoenix you are.

Once you have done that, you can manifest fiercely standing in your power. Trust me, you are powerful. How do you interpret feeling powerful? What does that mean to you? Do you feel excited about that or edgy? Our vibrations don't lie, it's an important step to accept and transform and honestly dive into what power and powerlessness look like to you. Remember – you are equal to anyone on this earth and have every right to rise.

Full Moon

Uncover the Mysteries: Power, Money, and Sex

Unless you've lived under a fairy's mushroom all your life, I'm sure you've heard that Scorpio is known for its sizzling sexuality. Scorpio oozes raw sensuality. The Scorpio Full Moon is the perfect time for an incredibly successful manifesting technique. Can you guess what it is? Yes, that's right, orgasm magic!

In early civilizations, sex was considered a sacred act. A respected profession was the sacred whore who, during sex, became the embodiment of the goddess and as such supernatural. A vessel for all things holy.

Tantric sex also talks about creating an energetic connection that is not just about the physical. The idea of using sexual energy for magical purposes goes back a long way. The Taoists wrote about it in 500 BCE. Napoleon Hill, the granddaddy of modern manifesting, in 1937 wrote in his famous book *Think and Grow Rich*:

> 'When harnessed and redirected along other lines, this motivating force [sex] maintains all of its attributes of keenness of imagination, courage, etc. which may be used as powerful creative forces in literature, art, or in any other profession or calling, including, of course, the accumulation of riches.'

When building your pleasure (alone or with someone else), visualize yourself surrounded by your successful manifestations, and at the time of climax, send your orgasm into the Universe, a calling signal to magnetize what you desire. Sexual magic is phenomenally successful, so be very careful what you wish for! Of course you can use this technique at any time, not just on the Full Moon. (If you're asexual, celibate, or not interested in this, you can transfer the technique to what I call a heart orgasm. Imagine a surge of love coming through your heart and radiating around the world, drawing to you your desire.)

SAGITTARIUS

New Moon

Manifesting Magic: Travel, Learning, Adventure

As the wild pony of the zodiac, Sagittarius brings adventure, expansion, and travel. The New Moon in this sign is a powerful catalyst for change, making it the perfect time to manifest a holiday, study, or embark on a wild adventure. This Moon can also bring unique and eccentric characters into our lives, reminding us to appreciate anyone who expresses freedom.

Use this time to unlock a journey to more independence and experience your free-spirited, feral side. You need to know that it is possible for you.

I mentioned the time I was a single parent living in a council flat with no money to pay for my electricity, yet I ended up flying to LA to stay in a hotel packed with celebrities. And taking my five-star trip to Tobago not long after. It is possible for you. Think about where your heart truly wants to go. Where is your soul compass pointing? What place would make your spirit sing?

Try this. Buy a postcard from the country of your choice (you can get them for pennies on eBay or Etsy), write it to yourself, and talk a little about the fun times you have had. Then, pop it on your fridge or a shelf where you can see it.

Full Moon

Learning, a Quest, Truth-telling

The Sagittarius Full Moon brings a burst of expansive energy – perfect for connecting with friends and embracing a spirit of exploration. Using Step Six (Embrace Co-Creation Power), schedule a Full Moon gathering so you can support each other's dreams. If you can't do this with friends, there are many online Moon groups. Find one that you feel is authentic, filled with like-minded people with big visions. This is a time for lively discussion, for sharing the ideas that inspire you, and for broadening your perspective, pulling in the Full Moon in Sagittarius's optimistic flair.

Something is being enhanced or expanded for you under this liberating and thrill-seeking Full Moon. Dreams of travel, adventure, or personal growth feel that much closer. Whether it's booking a long-awaited trip or mapping out a new learning path, use this lunar energy to fuel your intentions and visualize yourself taking those exhilarating first steps.

Your inner optimist is unleashed. Just a word of warning – seek out the fellow positive thinkers and adventurers under this Moon. You simply won't relate to anyone who focuses on the negative or thinks small. Remember those pre-steps and those parade rainers? Avoid under this Full Moon. Sagittarius is a sign that favors big, broad brush strokes. Don't worry about the details. That's the Universe's job. Yours is to answer the call toward something bigger.

CAPRICORN

New Moon

Wealth, Success, Achievements Fulfilled

The New Moon in Capricorn is our cosmic invitation to hike toward success, to manifest the achievements that truly matter. To release resistance and level up a new stage of ambition.

This is the Moon of money, status, and success, urging us to seek what we desire for financial security, job satisfaction, and the recognition we deserve. But Capricorn energy is also about the climb up the mountain of dreams itself. What needs to shift within you to reach that summit? What old beliefs or habits are holding you back?

As you step through this New Moon portal, dare to dream big. This is the time to allow the Universe to exceed your expectations, to deliver beyond what you thought possible. Whether it's a new job or a career move, or a commitment for personal growth, this is the lunar energy to harness as it's tenacious and never gives in. Prepare for your reputation to soar and for others to recognize your unique brilliance. Visualize the future surrounded by your achievements. Victory and triumph beckon.

Full Moon

Plan ahead for this Earthy Full Moon. Set yourself a list of intentions you plan to create and experience. Following the steps, it's crucial that you only set orders that you know and believe will arrive on the Full Moon. As you lead up to the event, count all your successes. Celebrate your wins and give yourself a pat on the back. The Full Moon in Capricorn is the perfect time to head out to a place where you feel you're thriving. Capricorns are persistent. They put their heads down and carry on until they get what they want. The Cappy secret is that they put one cloven hoof in front of the other until they get to the top of the mountain. Visualize yourself at the peak of success now.

This Full Moon can seek you out, putting you in the spotlight. Singling you out, thanks to the efforts you've been putting in. Going the distance brings you attention, rewards, and clear signs from the Universe or others that you're on the right path. Pause and receive your recognition. It will also show you just how fearlessly you've been removing any barriers to success that have held you back previously, as outlined in the steps. Who you are becoming, your own living success story, emerges for you. Work it!

190

AQUARIUS

New Moon

Congratulations! The Aquarius New Moon is the manifesting Moon of dreams. Aquarians are visionaries who thrive on visualizing and tuning into the future; they're also keenly aware that we're all connected as unique expressions of a greater whole. This New Moon empowers and amplifies our visions, connecting us to our highest potential.

A perfect time to light a white candle, write your desires into the candle with your fingernail, and visualize your soul lamp sparking up, seeing the rays of your desires circling the globe. Know that this is a powerful calling signal, that you are attracting the most fulfilling outcomes into your life. Your energy is connecting with all that there is, to bring coincidences, magic, and wonder toward you.

If you ever question your unique place in this grand design, remember that you are a vital part of a living, breathing Universe essential to its growth and evolution. We are all a single cell within a larger organism. Shed any doubts that may dim your light and recognize yourself as an essential thread in the intricate tapestry of existence. The Aquarius New Moon draws on those threads to bring the perfect connections.

While your candle is lit, open your journal and jot down headings of the things you want to manifest in this cycle. Under each heading tune into the Aquarius energy and the infinite knowledge available to you and write down three unique things you can do or express to draw your manifestations closer.

This New Moon is your most social and ripe with connectivity of the year. It sets the scene. Remember, it is via other people that the cosmos often channels our manifesting dreams. Connections and communities. And there's no better New Moon under which to go find yours. Remember – you matter in ways you cannot comprehend. Your unique soul has a pivotal role to play in setting events in motion which enable others to attain their desires. Just as they have one to play in yours. Find your people and make social manifesting part of your manifesto under this New Moon.

Full Moon

Just as the Aquarius New Moon sharpens our links to others, this social Full Moon wants us to connect, network (spiritually or literally), and collaborate. It's perfect for the group exercises like the Oprah interview above or any collaborative manifesting.

Gather a like-minded crew who want to join forces to manifest together. Whether it's a Zoom group online or a get-together in your home, the Aquarius Full Moon illuminates the power of unity. When we cheerlead each other's visions for the future and encourage and confirm our beliefs together, we amplify the magnetism.

As we visualize together, our force grows stronger. Use your group's power to send healing and strength to any part of the world that is in crisis and needs it. When we gather together, we become more contagious and can spread love. Aquarius Moon is a time not only for being a visionary but also giving back and supporting those around us.

Because Aquarius is the sign that rules our goals and dreams, this can often be a Full Moon under which one manifests. Or we begin to see real progress toward them. Someone can appear under this Full Moon who will have an as yet undisclosed role to play – so look out for who crosses your path or slides into those DMs. How you connect to others may also feature in some way. The more authentic, wild, and wonderful you are, the closer you get to your goal.

PISCES

New Moon

One of my favorite New Moons of the year, the Pisces New Moon exudes an otherworldly and magical vibe. Ruled by Neptune, Pisces operates on a deeper, intuitive level. If they were in an American high-school yearbook, Pisces would undoubtedly be voted 'Most likely to prove the existence of fairies'. Pisces' energy retains the essential childlike wonder so important to Step Three. The New Moon in Pisces asks you to open your heart to all the sweet, soft things your heart desires.

It's romantic and tender, dreamy and deliciously hopeful. If you're in a relationship, it's a great time to practice a little soft love magic where you place your left hand on each other's heart, look deeply into each other's eyes, and visualize all the things you want to manifest together. Be as giggly, starry-eyed, and dreamy as you like. Not into that? Why not make a manifesting pouch, knowing you possess all the magic you need for it to work beautifully?

Single in the New Moon in Pisces?
Our thoughts and beliefs are not only calling signals but also movies we play in our minds. We become casting directors, meticulously sorting the people in our lives into roles that fit our purpose.

What rom-coms have you been directing and starring in in this life? If we're seeking romance and meet someone who seems to tick all our boxes, in a flash we've cast them in a starring role, imagining a whirlwind of romantic scenarios. We might envision exciting dates, declarations of love, meeting friends and family, building a home together, and even strolling hand in hand on a beach at sunset. All this before we've even learned their last name. This fantasy can be intoxicating, but it often crumbles when reality sets in, revealing glaring incompatibilities, like discovering your vegan lifestyle clashes with their love of roast beef for breakfast.

The problem with immersing ourselves too deeply in this casting-director role is that it narrows our possibilities. Just as actors fear being typecast, limiting themselves to a single role, we too can restrict the potential connections in our lives by clinging to rigid expectations or repeating patterns. We are all multifaceted beings, brimming with potential waiting to be unleashed. It's important to let go of the control and start to understand, just like the sandwich mentioned earlier, the Universe can deliver a love that is outside our experience.

The Pisces New Moon invites us to release these self-imposed limitations and open our hearts to the magic that unfolds when we allow ourselves, and those around us, to shine in all our unique and unexpected ways. If you want to send out a calling signal for love, trust the Universe to send what is beyond your expectations.

Full Moon

It's emotional! The watery Full Moon brings up all our emotions. Our intuition is on full alert. We tend to feel sentimental. Music is a great enhancer of our emotions during a Full Moon in Pisces. Write your Manifesting Manifesto with your favorite empowering kick-ass tune in the background. Find a song or perhaps classical music that enhances your intentions.

Pay attention to your dreams on the Full Moon as they will be filled with treasure. Keeping a dream journal is like having a direct line to your inner magical, especially during the Pisces Full Moon when dreams are extra potent and vivid. I've been journaling my dreams since I was a child and it's been a game-changer, just like learning to read Tarot or any other divination tool. The more you tune into your dreams, the clearer their messages become.

The night before and on the night of the Full Moon in Pisces, ask for a dream that reveals your future, solves a problem, or gives you key information on how to heal. Then grab a note-book and pen, or even better your phone's voice recorder, and keep them close to your bed. As soon as you wake up, jot down or record everything you remember, even if it's just snippets.

Our brains are notorious for forgetting dreams quickly, so don't delay. If you wake up in the middle of the night, write those dreams down too, as they often have different vibes than the ones we have closer to morning.

When reading your dream journal, pay attention to the sym-bols, colors, and emotions that stand out. Write them down on a fresh page, describing them as if you're explaining them to a friend who's never heard of them before. Let's say you dreamed about a sheep. You might write, 'It's a fluffy, four-legged animal with curly wool. They live in flocks and say "baa".'

By breaking down your dreams like this, you can uncover hidden meanings and gain surprising insights. It's like your subconscious is sending you secret messages and this is how you decode them. You can do this every night, not just on the Full Moon. Over time, you'll start to recognize patterns and recurring symbols, making it easier to decipher what your dreams are trying to tell you. Soon enough, you'll know the difference between a treasure map to your future, a warning dream, a prophetic vision, and a sweet hello from your spirit guides or loved ones.

CONCLUSION

I hope reading this book gives you the deepest compassion for yourself, for your past, and for your process. Without knowing how to filter the energy, opinions, and ideas bombarding us since birth, we've all been held in an invisible prison. Our divine and sacred spark has been hijacked by the culture and society we grew up in. Illusions have compromised our potential, yet the power of you has always been here.

We live in a world more mysterious and magical than we can possibly know. Once we embrace our power and acknowledge the truth hiding in plain sight – that we are each a unique spark of creation, connected to the infinite whole – we no longer need to be tossed around by circumstances or other people's contagious ideas. It is then that we awaken to our true potential and we can craft our own thrilling destiny. A destiny we wholeheartedly deserve. I wish you success and happiness beyond your wildest dreams. I believe in you, the cosmos believes in you, and your destiny is yours to create.

So much love to you, Michele x

TROUBLESHOOTING

Is it time for a manifesting health check? Or just to go deeper into why you want what you want? Are dastardly doubts already creeping in? Are you feeling less sure about your results than you were when you read the chapter on your manifesto? If this book is a manual, then you have arrived at the troubleshooting section. And it's not just about those FAQs. It's also about the old, frequently encountered speed bumps. The ones that slowed or stalled you in the past. This time, however, you're prepared.

Troubleshooting Tips

Time for some manifestation myth busting! There's so much stuff out there when it comes to the how and why of manifesting. And chances are, if you have this book in your hand, you've been caught out by the fake manifesting news. Which is why, despite all your bravery and hard work, you've gotten mixed results in the past.

Then of course there's the point where we may feel that we're stalled. Nothing much seems to be happening. We begin to question ourselves and the process. Are we doing anything wrong? Or, just like a Mercury-retrograde glitch on our device, do we just need a troubleshooting manual to reboot our intention? The answers to those FAQs we will all find ourselves asking at some point? Or just an explanation of where we've veered off course without knowing it?

Just for fun, I thought I'd call them the **Lies of Attraction** – because they are things that we can buy into as being absolutely true, necessary, and right when that isn't the case at all. Or they can lie in wait and trip us up again when we least expect it. So here are the lies – and the truth behind them exposed.

1. **My destiny is set in stone.** This is a great big lumpen lie that can cause you to choke if you swallow it. The idea that we are powerless and cannot change our path. We all have some experiences that are fated to come our way. But our destiny is in our hands and it's shaped by evolving who we are and how we handle whatever comes.

   The idea that your destiny is fixed and that you have no say in it can lead you to think that you are a victim of fate rather than a creator of it. It can also lead to a 'Why bother?' mindset. After all, if you don't have any influence over what happens to you, what's the point of even trying to manifest your dreams? Or there was one 'predestined' moment where you missed the boat because you were at the airport instead! The truth is that we are powerful creators, actually here to evolve into our power, and that in itself shapes our destiny.

2. **I create and attract from my mind.** A lot of what I share with you involves working at a mental level, but actually you create from multiple levels of your being. These levels go up as far as your spiritual connection to the whole of the Universe and down to your root chakra, which connects you to the earth and is the energy center in our body, associated in part with safety and its shadow, fear.

   I focus a lot on the mind, getting you to do mental exercises such as meditation or working with affirmations, because the mind needs to be engaged and stimulated and your creativity needs to be fired up and sent in constructive directions. But it really doesn't run the show. You are at your most powerful when all aspects of you are in total alignment. Trying to create from the mind when your heart isn't engaged or when your soul isn't in it is a much slower and more laborious process. So, your mind has a key role to play – but not the only one.

3. **I need to be very specific about every detail of how everything is going to work out.** Magic doesn't do minutiae. This is actually something that your mind may get hung up on, but it really isn't necessary at all to deliver your results. Because no matter how bold your imagination is or how big your vision for yourself, I can guarantee the Universe can come up with something better. So, leave it space to do just that.

   I actively encourage people to go beyond their mind into limitless potential purely because your imagination is pretty powerful, but it's only really a patch on the magnificence that exists in this abundant Universe. This is really down to how you want to play it. I've manifested things by using detail, such as my holiday in Tobago. But it's also fun to say, this is the energy of what I want to experience and I'll leave the details to the cosmos.

   On a more serious note, being insistent on the detail can actually be a bit of control-freakery playing out and that's a low-level vibration to be working at.

4. **I can only be happy when I've got what I want.** You can be totally happy with what you have even as you are working on attracting something in – and in fact it's important that you are. We all get down and a bit desperate at times, and you know from your own experience what a low vibration that is and how hard it is to be a conscious creator from that space.

Sometimes I see people who are so focused on the myth that they will only be happy when they land a particular job or attract a particular relationship into their lives that they fail to realize this is the very mindset that is stopping that from manifesting. The truth is that when you are happy, vibrant, and positive about everything as it is right now, you are putting out the most powerful attractor force and things flow more easily. And if you suddenly realize you have bought into this fake manifesting myth – the good news is that this book contains the myth-busting exercise to counteract that!

To Get the Figs, Let Go of the Figs

Did you ever come across the Aesop's fable about the monkey who stuck his hand in a jar of figs, but when he grabbed a handful of the fruit his fist was too large to pull it out through the neck again? He was left dancing in rage with the jar dangling from his arm, unable to get what he wanted and unable to let go.

Aesop was a slave in Ancient Greece with an astonishing grasp of human nature. Like all good stories, we can interpret this one in a number of ways. Like the Four of Cups in the Tarot where we see a figure intently staring at three cups with an air of 'Meh ...' – completely unaware that there is a bigger and more tantalizing fourth cup being offered. How often do we get so emotionally invested in one outcome that we cut ourselves off from other possibilities that could be so much better?

To an outsider, it seems obvious that all the monkey has to do is let go of the figs, remove his paw, and then upend the jar so that the fruit falls out. Simple. There is always more than one way to reach our goal. Some may be a lot easier than others. And whether we realize it at the time or not, there may also be other outcomes which not only can hand us what we think our goal will deliver but may in fact be easier to attain and give us a lot more.

This is why, from a manifesting perspective, I always suggest we hold our intentions – but remain flexible. Not only in how they get delivered but in not worrying about the how and the why. We just naturally assume they will be. To remain open as to their final form. Which leads me to my next troubleshooting tip.

Be Open
This is linked to what we began in Step Four (Order With the Joy and Expectation of a Child). But it's your troubleshooting hack for when you may have questions about whether or not your delivery has arrived.

Yes, you're secure now in your practice and the knowledge that what you have asked for will manifest. Then, something appears – but it doesn't quite look the way you expected it to. One example of this would be you have decided that you want to set up your own business. You've created your lifeline. Honed your focus to laser precision. And are fully engaged in doing what you can in the present to bring your vision into being. Not just that vision board but that business plan, research, or even upskilling. Then, out of the blue, a former contact offers you an opportunity to join their business. Do you accept or knock back the offer to continue to invest in your own dream and remain true to your goal?

Discover 'What If?'
Remember what we've said about how the Universe can always dream bigger? There's an ancient saying: all paths lead to the top of the mountain. What matters is that we are focused on the goal of getting to the top, NOT the route we take to get there.

Ordering with the trust of a child means if an alternative or even more scenic path to the top appears, we take it, provided it excites us. We are willing to discover what lies along it. So, to return to the above example, accepting the offer does not mean you are abandoning your goal of starting your own business. On the contrary, it may be the Universe's path to doing exactly that.

By deciding to find out what could be waiting along that route, you could encounter people who become pivotal in helping you achieve this. You could even gain knowledge, experience, or skills that you can incorporate into your own business which end up being key factors in its success that you would not have discovered if you had not said yes in the first place. And you had a great time doing it. You also enabled your contact to manifest their vision and became part of their power-group dynamic – engaging with the co-creator principle – which in turn super-boosts your own manifesting journey.

When we're children, we're naturally curious about the world. We're not yet in the mindset where we've been brainwashed to believe there's only one right way to do something. By letting go, being willing to explore and find out what lies down that alternative route, we not only link back to our magical curiosity and willingness to wonder 'What if ...?', we harness the joy and expectation that fuel effortless manifestation. Understanding that well – the Universe works in mysterious ways – is all part of that.

Be willing to explore as opportunities, like angels, can visit in disguise. The only caveat is that it has to excite you and have the potential to take you someplace new in terms of experience. Short cuts to our dreams often mean going off-road!

Change your Metaphor – Change your Life

Researchers at Stanford University set out to explore how the metaphors used when talking about crime affected responses to it. In one experiment, 485 participants were divided into two groups. Both groups were presented with exactly the same statistic related to crime but the metaphors used to talk about it differed.

One group saw a passage that talked about the crimes being a virus 'infecting' a city. The other saw the same figures, but this time crime was talked about as being a beast that was 'preying' on the city. People taking part in the research were asked to read the paragraph they were given and suggest what could be done to reduce crime. The researchers found that the group given the virus metaphor leaned toward delving into the root causes and tackling the social problems that led to crime. Suggestions by those given the beast metaphor talked about fighting back and increasing the number of police officers to catch and 'cage' criminals.

Think about the metaphors that might spring to your mind right now in relation to a situation you want to change. Especially if this involves someone you know. Or even a group of people. If you're not getting on with someone and you think about them as being a 'pain in the neck' or they 'piss you off', what are you likely to want to do as a result?

There's a saying: bless your enemy, for they are the agent of your transformation. Now imagine your response if you see them as a soul connection. Someone who has come along to help you evolve. Or how about if you see them as a bundle of psychic energy that either is or isn't in alignment with your psychic energy? How simply opening yourself up to even considering that not only stops it being so personal but also instantly takes you out of reacting mode.

No, of course you don't have to put up with someone's hurtful or disrespectful behavior. Or agree with them. You have just consciously opted to change the metaphor to find the growth. And the optimal inner state for you.

Notice what shifts happen when you play around with the metaphors you use. You'll discover they color your emotions and influence your actions. Struggling with a problem? Examine your metaphors. Reframing them could revolutionize your approach. Words are spells. Words aren't just words – they build the blueprints for how we experience and navigate our world. This is life changing, not only for our day-to-day reality but also to enhance and refine our manifesting skills. And our people ones too.

When we embrace and understand how powerful words are, we can pay careful attention to how we use them, how they conjure our reality, and, yes, influence our interactions.

DISCOVER THE OFFICIAL
KNIGHT-WAITE TAROT DECK

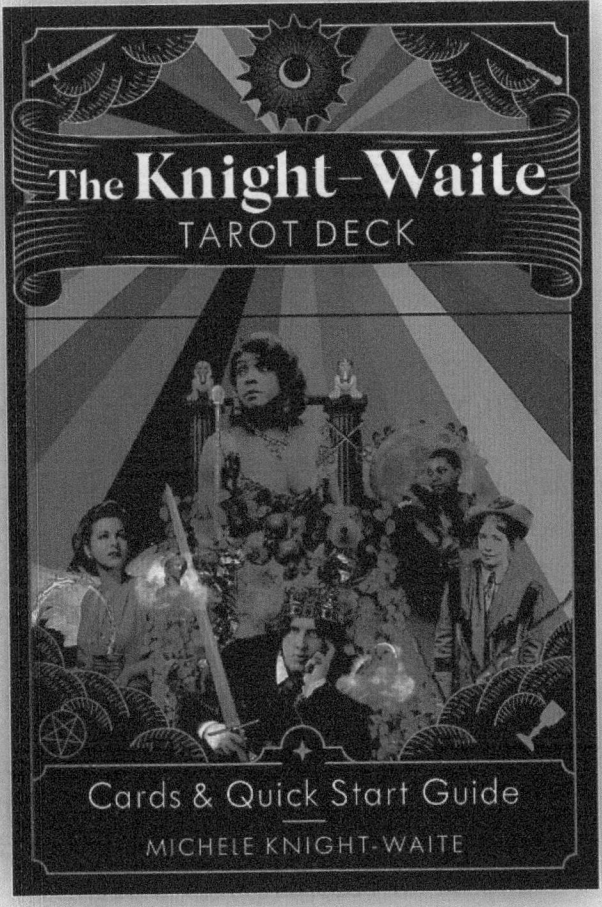

The Knight-Waite Tarot Guidebook

Using this guide alongside your Tarotdeck will help you
tune in to the story the cards are telling you, enjoying
wisdom and support right when you need it. Together
with your cards, this book will open the door to your
higher intuition and reveal astonishing truths about
yourself, your life, and the people around you.

The Knight-Waite Tarot Guidebook features
full interpretations of every card in the deck, sample
spreads showing different ways to conduct a reading,
and space for recording your thoughts.

ISBN 978 1 399 80736 4